Scenes from Canadian Plays

● ● ●

SCENES FROM CANADIAN PLAYS

● ● ●

From Automatic Pilot to Zastrozzi

Edited by
Dwayne Brenna

With an Introduction
by Mavor Moore

FIFTH HOUSE PUBLISHERS
Saskatoon Saskatchewan

Canadian Catologuing in Publication Data
Brenna, Dwayne, editor 1955-
Scenes from Canadian Plays
ISBN 0-920079-45-8
1. Canadian drama (English) - 20th century
I. Brenna, Dwayne, 1955-
PS8307.s346 1989 C812'.5 C89-098042-X
PR9196.3.S346 1989

This book has been published with the assistance of
The Saskatchewan Arts Board and The Canada Council.

Designed by Robert MacDonald, MediaClones Inc.,
Saskatoon Saskatchewan and Toronto Ontario.

To Wilson Gustav Brenna and his mother.

Special thanks to the following people, who contributed to the making
of this book: Rhoda Miko, Beverley Brenna, Ronald Mavor, Herbert
Berry, my students in Drama 112 and 212 at the University of
Saskatchewan and, mostly, the fine playwrights featured herein.

Fifth House Publishers
20 – 36th Street East
Saskatoon, Saskatchewan
S7K 5S8

Printed in Canada

CONTENTS

(Scenes are for two characters except where noted.)

Introduction

Four justifications are usually advanced for publishing selections of short scenes from longer plays. The samples offer the reader a sort of shopping list, designed, like the midway barker's rundown, to make you lust after the rest of the show. They provide an overview of a range of subjects and styles impossible to attain in a single volume of complete work weighing less than 10 kilograms. They are extremely useful in acting training, where art is long and classes short. And they are absolutely essential to auditions.

Since there already exist several anthologies of scenes in English, however, a new selection from Canadian plays needs a few more justifications. They are not hard to find, but like everything else Canadian they tend to be a little apologetic when introduced. The most important of them, I believe, have no easy parallel in the British, European or American traditions.

The first is that only recently - since the Second World War - have we had either a past or a present dramatic literature. Our professional theater (mistakenly believed by many to have arrived with the Stratford Festival in 1953) began as early as that of the United States, but original plays were few, the published ones even fewer. It was, after all, a small market. Only after the fame achieved by Canadian radio drama in the 1940s, the international acceptance of our theater's professionalism in the '50s and '60s, and the appearance of a substantial cadre of playwrights in the '70s, was interest in our theatrical past aroused and the recall of its achievements begun.

Consequently the general public (and, regrettably, many a teacher) is not yet aware of the cultural resource at hand. The present anthology, if used as widely as it deserves, will help to dispel that self-defeating blindness.

The plays date from Gwen Pharis Ringwood's 1938 *Still Stands the House* to some of the most recent experimental works, and cover a wide range - the only way to cover Canada - of style, approach and setting. Among others, I miss representation from James Reaney, our best dramatic poet, from Beverly Simon, still our best absurdist, and from John Herbert - whose *Fortune and Men's Eyes* remains our single biggest international commercial success, unless one counts the expatriate Bernard Slade *(Same Time, Next Year)* as a Canadian playwright. But I know there are often copyright problems, among others, and I stand amazed at what Dwayne Brenna has been able to get into his collection.

A second particular justification is that Canadians, lacking a single tradition, have long had three (Native, French and British) and now have many more. One cannot talk about the Canadian drama in

English without including translations from other tongues. One of the earliest plays in this collection, Gratien Gélinas' quebecois *Tit-Coq* (1948), had as much impact on Canadian theater as any play written in English - partly because it was a great success here in both languages, partly because it was the first Canadian production of a Canadian play in either language to go to Broadway, partly because it flopped on Broadway and taught us to pit our own judgment against that of the experts from out of town.

The present collection indicates most of the cultural streams that together make up what would be known elsewhere as a mainstream - everything from a Native playwright (Highway) to Québec dramatists (Tremblay, Dubois) to those, such as Ryga, with more recent immigrant backgrounds. Even a couple of American converts get into the act.

Still another justification for this Canadian anthology is that it provides exercises in our own idioms. Our actors have become so used to disguising themselves as British or American for the purpose of appearing in British and American films and plays - or in British and American translations of European plays - that they have to work hard at reclaiming their own accents when needed. While this chameleon-like skill develops versatility in our performers, it puts them at a disadvantage in terms of naturalistic acting, and in terms of establishing a rapport with their audiences.

For our actors to perform before Canadian audiences in British dialect (with all its class baggage), in a British adaptation of Sophocles, Moliere, Ibsen or Chekhov only puts another barrier between play and public. It also fortifies the prejudice that "good" classical speech, no matter how unEnglish the classic, requires copying the accents of modern London - a bias the English theater long ago abandoned. The parallel prejudice that "good" naturalistic North American speech (like "good" pop singing) requires some sort of US accent is equally reductionist.

The price of versatility is anonymity. And audiences who cannot see themselves reflected in a mirror are not likely to hold the mirror in much esteem. This anthology will help artists, teachers and public to see the reflection. I welcome it.

Mavor Moore, CC, Vancouver, 1989

AUTOMATIC PILOT

Erika Ritter

Place: Charlie's apartment in Toronto
Time: the present, late summer
Characters: Charlie, 30; Gene, 23

Charlie is a writer for television soaps and an aspiring comedienne at a comedy club called the Canada Goose. As other characters in the play maintain, Charlie does her best comedic work when she is unhappy. And unhappiness is in good supply: her husband of eight years, an actor, "came out of the closet" a year ago and moved to Stratford; and she has had a recent affair with Nick, an uncommitted "70s" rake, who jilted her at lunch earlier in the day.

Nick's younger brother Gene shows up at Charlie's apartment that evening. Charlie has been drinking copious amounts of wine. As the scene begins, she is sitting on her bed, singing the Esso "Happy Motoring" song into the mike on her tape recorder. Gene enters, unnoticed by Charlie. He helps her finish the song, then admonishes her for not locking her door.

GENE: Aren't you going to ask me how I got in?
CHARLIE: Chargex, American Express - what's the difference?
GENE: The door's open, that's how. Charlie, it's late. Don't you ever lock it?
CHARLIE: Is that what brings you here? A survey on the Imprudent Habits of Single Women?
GENE: They missed you down at The Canada Goose tonight.
CHARLIE: What were you doing at the club?
GENE: I knew you were on tonight.
CHARLIE: Yeah? How did I do? *(Laughs, but he doesn't join in)*
GENE: When I got there, Mel was trying to get you on the phone to find out where the hell you were. *(Goes to the phone, examines the disconnected jack)* Out, I see.

CHARLIE: In a manner of speaking.

GENE: Anyway, I was worried.

CHARLIE: And you rushed right over, in the hopes of being the first to say, "I told you so." *(Indicates wastebasket)* Congratulations. You made it.

GENE: Roses. Jesus.

CHARLIE: You want to look at the card?

GENE: *(Looks her in the eye)* "No regrets. No blame. No bitterness." Something along those lines?

CHARLIE: *(After a pause)* Say, did I ever tell you the one about the dumb broad, the professional bastard and the professional bastard's know-it-all younger brother?

GENE: Let me tell you one. Nick never promised you anything. So you've come out ahead. If you count the flowers as a bonus.

CHARLIE: Don't you stick up for him.

GENE: He's my brother, Charlie. He has his faults, and I'm sorry if he hurt you. But he tried to play straight with you and you know it.

CHARLIE: Am I supposed to thank you for pointing that out?

GENE: No, but you could offer me a drink.

CHARLIE: Not if you've come here to gloat.

GENE: No.

CHARLIE: In that case, have a drink. *(Unscrews the top from the last bottle of wine)* Care to smell the cap?

GENE: Where did all these bottles come from?

CHARLIE: The liquor store sends their empties over. I'm too young to drink, of course. But I like my garbage to look adult.

GENE: *(Takes a swig of wine)* My favorite. Melted cough drops.

CHARLIE: If you don't like the house wine, don't blame me. I stole it from my neighbor. He's out of town and I'm feeding his cat. Of course, we can always try our luck with the neighbor on the other side. I'm watering her plants. *(Shakes a key ring)* The keys to the kingdom, baby.

GENE: How much of this did you drink tonight?

CHARLIE: All of it.

GENE: All of it? Holy shit. Charlie are you all right?

CHARLIE: Never better. Oh, the day's had its ups and downs, I don't deny it. But I'm feeling better now. I had a good cry, I guess, and a little nap, and now I'm even working on the act. *(Switches on the tape, sings into the mike)* "You can trust the products at the Esso sign - " *(But as GENE regards her steadily, she switches off the tape)* Oh, well, a little later, maybe. *(Close to tears)* After a cigarette. You got one, by any chance?

GENE: *(Hands her a cigarette)* You're in no mood to work on the act now.

CHARLIE: I know. But maybe that's no excuse.

GENE: Charlie, that doesn't make much sense.

CHARLIE: I don't know. I was thinking tonight, about this comic they brought up from L.A. one time to headline at The Canada Goose. There was this one night, the show hadn't gone very well at all. And he invited three or four of the comics - young guys and me - back to his hotel room. He said he wanted to smoke dope and forget about the way the act had gone. But you know what happened when we got back to the hotel room?

GENE: What?

CHARLIE: The headliner brought out the dope all right, but while the rest of us smoked it and watched the gangsters on the Late Late Show, the comic just sat in a corner, all alone, and played the tapes of his act. The room was a mess - dried up old pizza crusts and coffee cups and cigarette butts. But the comic just sat there in the mess, with a stop-watch, and a notepad, and played the tapes.

GENE: So what did the rest of you do?

CHARLIE: What could we do? He WAS the headliner from L.A. So after every line, somebody would say, "That's a funny bit, man. That's very funny." And gradually the headliner began to pay attention to the fact that we were there, and he started throwing out new lines he'd spun off from the stuff on the tape. And after every line, he'd stop and ask, "What about THAT? Could THAT be funny?" Some of it was funny and some of it wasn't, but we told him it was dynamite and he wrote it down. I think that he was afraid that if he stopped, he'd die. You know, the way a shark has to keep moving or die? I think he was afraid that if he stopped, he'd be consumed by the garbage in the hotel room, or the ambition of the young comics coming up behind him, or the brutality of the Late Late Show.

GENE: But he was the one who messed up the room. He was the one who invited you in, and turned on the TV.

CHARLIE: That's right. *(Pause)* I wonder. Maybe he actually NEEDED the awfulness around him for incentive. Maybe he needed some place like that, that he HAD to be funny in or die.

GENE: Could be.

CHARLIE: So, maybe this is no time for ME to stop. Maybe I've got to keep going now, or die.

(GENE clicks on the tape recorder, speaks into the mike)

GENE: Charlie, you're not going to die. Not tonight, anyway. *(Clicks it off.)* There. Now you've got it on tape. Play it back whenever you need reassurance.

CHARLIE: That's the worst part of being a comedian. Everybody just laughs at you. *(As GENE laughs)* See what I mean?

GENE: You're priceless. You really are.

CHARLIE: You're not so bad yourself. I've always liked you, Gene.

GENE: Now, there's a case of revisionist history.

CHARLIE: After that first morning, I mean. And you were right. To give me a word of warning.

GENE: It could be worse. You could be in love with him.

CHARLIE: Who says I'm not?

GENE: I do. What do you say?

CHARLIE: *(After a pause)* No. I toyed with the possibility, while we were in the restaurant today and I realized he was looking for a way to kiss me off. I came very close to being in love with him, out of pure spite. But I'm not. It's more of a fascination, I guess. How anybody with so many connections can be so unconnected to anything. Women fall for stuff like that.

GENE: Yeah? I'll make a note of it.

CHARLIE: No, don't. Don't you turn into one of those half-assed '70s people. There are enough of them already. I guess we used up our quota of commitment in the '60s. Now we always keep our options open, as my late husband would say.

GENE: And what does he mean by that?

CHARLIE: Someday, sonny, when you're older, you'll understand.

GENE: Do you?

CHARLIE: No.

GENE: Then you're not one of those people, either, are you?

CHARLIE: Gene, why did you come here tonight?

GENE: I never miss a chance to sing the Happy Motoring Song.

CHARLIE: Is that all?

GENE: I like you, Charlie. I always have.

CHARLIE: Now, there's a case of revisionist history.

GENE: Seriously, from the first minute I saw you. I said to myself, "Now there's a woman I could quit law school for."

CHARLIE: Bullshit. You quit law school to become the greatest novelist the world has ever known. You told me so yourself.

GENE: Charlie, you've got to learn to take a compliment.

CHARLIE: I want to know why you came here.

GENE: You mean did Nick send me? No.

CHARLIE: You mean he's not in the habit of passing along his old girlfriends? Like hockey skates? I wouldn't put it past him.

GENE: You ought to think a little better of me.

CHARLIE: I'm sorry.

GENE: So am I.

CHARLIE: Are you?

GENE: Sorry. *(Kisses her)* Sorry. *(Kisses her again)* Sorry. *(And again. CHARLIE pulls away)* Uh ... that's not exactly how I planned my move.

CHARLIE: This isn't quite how I saw today shaping up, either.

GENE: Charlie, this may come as a surprise to you, but you're not a pair of hockey skates.

CHARLIE: Is that one of those compliments I'm supposed to learn how to take?

GENE: If I'd wanted wisecracks, I'd have stayed at The Canada Goose.

CHARLIE: And if I'd wanted to save my sanity, I'd have stayed away from the Bolton boys.

GENE: I'm not one of the Bolton boys. I'm Gene. And what went wrong with you and Nick has nothing to do with me.

CHARLIE: You mean, don't throw out the baby with the bathwater? *(Suddenly laughs)* Oh, God, I'm sorry ... *(Still laughing)* I just realized what I said.

GENE: *(Sharply)* Charlie, I said cut the cracks. I'm not a baby and I'm not the relief pitcher, or any other goddamn thing you think. And if you had any kind of decent opinion of yourself, I wouldn't have to tell you that.

CHARLIE: *(Stares at him uncertainly)* Gene ... do you want to sleep with me?

GENE: It's crossed my mind. From time to time. To time.

CHARLIE: Why?

GENE: What kind of a question is that?

CHARLIE: I mean, why am I not a pair of hockey skates?

GENE: *(Earnestly)* Listen to me. I don't make a habit of chasing around after the recently broken-hearted, knocking on the door -

CHARLIE: You DIDN'T knock -

GENE: Knocking on the door and offering myself as the consolation prize. You attract me, all right? You always have. In spite of your neuroses and your bad taste in men and your habit of calling my "sonny." And right now, I can't think of anything nicer than being in bed with you. I can't see how it can fail as a bright idea.

CHARLIE: But?

GENE: I didn't say but.

CHARLIE: You were thinking but. I saw it, in one of those balloons, over your head.

GENE: But I'm not like Nick and all the open-option people. Gene. The name is Gene. I want you to have that straight in the morning. And the morning after. And the morning after that. What do you say, Charlie?

(CHARLIE switches on the tape, picks up the mike)

CHARLIE: *(Into the mike)* Gene. I have it straight. And I'll have it straight in the morning. *(Clicks off the tape)* There. Now you've got it on tape. Play it back when you need reassurance. *(Takes off her glasses)* Your turn. Fair is fair.

(GENE takes off his glasses, then picks up CHARLIE's looks through them)

GENE: You're as blind as I am.

CHARLIE: This could be the beginning of a beautiful friendship.

(She leans towards him, and he kisses her on a blackout)

BABEL RAP

John Lazarus

Place: the highest point on the Tower of Babel
Time: unspecified, but modern dress recommended
Characters: Worker, Smoker

High atop the Tower of Babel (in the first production, the edifice was
suggested by a step-ladder), the Smoker and the Worker contemplate
the nature of God. The Smoker has been content, through the play's
early scenes, to sit back and watch as the Worker builds upwards,
towards God's heaven. Does God appreciate man's struggle for
perfection, symbolized by the construction of the Tower? Or does He
spurn such industry as mortal man's pretentious attempt to raise
himself to the level of divine power? Worker and Smoker are faced
with these questions as they try to justify their respective attitudes—
the Smoker his inactivity, the Worker his ambition. The following
scene begins after the Smoker asks, "Who do you think He'll like
best?"

WORKER: I sing hymns to Him. I'm always singing hymns to Him.
SMOKER: I've noticed.
WORKER: You never sing hymns to Him.
SMOKER: Don't jump to conclusions. Maybe I sing them silently.
WORKER: Well, I sing mine nice and loud. I'm not ashamed of mine.
I'll bet He really enjoys mine.
SMOKER: Does He.
WORKER: *(Starting low and sweet and unctuously pious)*
Holy, holy, holy,
Lord God Almighty,
Early in the morning
Our song shall rise to Thee ...
SMOKER: *(Ditto, but a bit louder; he overlaps the WORKER's hymn,
beginning during the line "Early in the morning")*
The Lord's my shepherd,
I'll not want,
He makes me down to lie
In pastures green,
He leadeth me
The quiet waters by ...

WORKER: *(Again raising the volume a bit; having been interrupted, he takes revenge by starting on the SMOKER'S line "In pastures green")*
Mine eyes have seen the Glory of the coming of the Lord,
He is trampling through the vintage where the grapes of wrath are stor'd;
He hath loos'd the fearful lightning of His terrible swift sword,
His truth is ...

SMOKER: *(Swinging, jiving, snapping his fingers, coming in somewhere around "fearful lightning")*
Swing low, sweet chariot,
Coming for to carry me home,
Swing low, sweet chariot,
Comin' for to carry me ...

WORKER: *(Full volume, grand opera, all stops out; tune from Handel's "Messiah")*
Hallelujah! Hallelujah!
Hallelujah, Hallelujah, Halle-e-lu-jaahh!
For the Lord God Omni-i-potent reigneth ...

SMOKER: *(Half singing along, half shouting)*
Hallelujah! Hallelujah!

SMOKER and WORKER: *(Screaming at each other in fury)*
Hallelujah! Hallelujah! Hallelujah!
(They are suddenly interrupted by a huge and angry thunderclap and a profound dimming and flickering of the lights. The two stop and look up for a moment, and then dive for a hiding place - in the original production, the two actors had worked their way to the top of the step-ladder during the hymn sequence, and at this point scurried down the ladder again to cower on a small platform built across its lower struts. At any rate, they hide, quaking and gazing up at the storm, which rumbles and flickers for several moments before it slowly dies out in a sulky muttering and rumbling. The lights become steady, but at a somewhat dimmer level than the bright sunshine we had before. A silent pause)

SMOKER: *(With awe and fear)* Maybe we should cut out the bullshit ...

WORKER: *(With awe and fear)* I don't think He's too pleased with either one of us at the moment.

SMOKER: He probably feels we're presuming.

WORKER: *(Frustrated)* Yes, but presuming to what? Presuming to find favor with the Almighty? What's wrong with that?

SMOKER: Well, maybe we shouldn't be putting each other down in order to do it.

WORKER: *(With some self-pity)* Perhaps ... I wish He'd tell us what the hell He wants from us. I mean, I'm doing my best.

SMOKER: I know; it's very trying.

WORKER: Trying is the word for it.

SMOKER: Hey, maybe He just wants us to co-operate. Get along. Work together.

WORKER: Work together? Huh. I know what that means. That's where I came in. With me working and you goofing off.

SMOKER: No, no, I don't mean just on the Tower. I mean on anything. He may not want us to work on the Tower at all. But if we're going to work on something, maybe He figures we shouldn't fight over it.

WORKER: Okay. Well. What is there to work on?

SMOKER: I dunno.

WORKER: Look. As I pointed out a short time ago, you might as well work on the Tower as on anything else. Helps pass the time.

SMOKER: Hm.

WORKER: *(His idea gaining momentum)* And ... judging from that little thunder routine, He is perfectly capable of expressing His displeasure when He wants to. Ergo, He hasn't previously wanted to ... ergo, the Tower is an acceptable project on which to work.

SMOKER: *(Considers this for a moment)* Maybe He didn't know we were around until just now.

WORKER: What?

SMOKER: We were singing pretty loudly. Maybe our singing attracted His attention. Maybe He hadn't noticed us before.

WORKER: How could He not have noticed us before? He sees the little sparrow fall ... We're building the tallest goddamn Tower in human history! I'm hammering nails at top volume. You're letting cigarette smoke drift up into the stratosphere. How could He not have noticed us?

SMOKER: Maybe He was asleep. *(Pause)*

WORKER: *(Horrified)* Do you think maybe we woke Him up?

SMOKER: It's a possibility.

WORKER: That's not a very nice thing to do, is it?

SMOKER: Well, if I were the Almighty, trying to get some sleep, and two guys were building a tower and singing hymns one floor below me, I imagine I might get mildly pissed off. *(Pause)*

WORKER: Maybe we should apologize.

SMOKER: Maybe we should.

(They kneel side by side in attitudes of prayer. They pray ad lib, almost silently, in very low whispers, but we can see their mouths moving, and they tend to gesture. Their approach vacillates between abject flattery and high-pressure persuasion)

SMOKER: *(Finishing first)* Amen ...

(The WORKER goes on, ad lib; we can barely hear him, but it sounds like he is blaming the noise on the SMOKER)

Amen!!

WORKER: Amen. *(Pause. They look around. WORKER, conspiratorially)* Any reply?

SMOKER: No. You?

WORKER: No ... He never says nothin' to me anyway.

(The lights have been brightening back to sunlight)

SMOKER: Well, maybe we calmed Him down a little. The sun's shining ... everything seems all right!

WORKER: *(With apparent heartiness, but underneath a new unease)* Yeah! Everything ... seems the same ... *(Brief pause)*

SMOKER: Well! I'm gonna have another cigarette.

WORKER: Right! You do that. I'm gonna ... get back to work ... Shalom.

SMOKER: Shazam. *(The WORKER does not move)* Something wrong?

WORKER: You know there's something wrong.

SMOKER: Yeahh ... Hey, do you get the feeling we're being watched? *(As soon as the thought is voiced, the two look frantically around them. They look high and low, upstage and into the audience, and wind up looking back at one another)*

WORKER: Nobody around.

SMOKER: Nope.

WORKER: Just ... you and me! Heh, heh.

SMOKER: Yup.

WORKER: We are definitely being watched.

SMOKER: *(Equally nervous, but a bit more in control)* Yes. Definitely. There's somebody behind us.

WORKER: *(Starting to panic)* How can there be somebody behind us? We're facing each other!

SMOKER: Yeah! I know ...

(Pause as they both realize the identity of the watcher)

WORKER: Look busy. *(Handing the SMOKER a tool)* Here. Get to work.

SMOKER: Right. *(They both get to work, whistling ostentatiously. They work for a few moments, still paranoid; a couple of touches of thunder)* Hey, will ya pass the gerzil?

WORKER: *(Preoccupied)* What?

SMOKER: Kindly pass the gerzil. *(Brief pause)*

WORKER: What the fump is a gerzil? *(Brief pause)*

SMOKER: The gerzil, you plink! It's in the gool fronk.

(Pause. All work has stopped)

WORKER: Are ... you playing some kind of a shnobbly frape with me? What is this crimple? *(Pause)*

SMOKER: What the fnerch are you scroggling about?

WORKER: All right, come on, nerkle. Flumb it.

SMOKER: Aw, cub it ouch!

(Pause as the WORKER seethes for a moment; then he loses his temper)

WORKER: I have had enunch! You blaw gap futhermudding summon a fitch!

SMOKER: Why you cog spugging hansard! Don't you spall me grames!

WORKER: Plimp!

SMOKER: Grutch!

WORKER: *(Grabbing the SMOKER by his collar)* Chiltz!

SMOKER: *(Doing likewise)* Patser! *(A sudden blast of thunder. The lights dim again. SMOKER, realizing, points to the sky)* See? See? It's Hib! It's Gob! He's blogging argle! Befuzz we're gilding the Townsend! He's mailing us gawk funny!

WORKER: I stan't undercand a flerd you snay! You're glonking funny!

SMOKER: *(Overlapping slightly)* I stan't undercand a flerd you snay! You're glonking funny!

(Thunder up. They look at the sky. The SMOKER suddenly starts pulling out planks, and throwing them down. Thunder under)

WORKER: You can't doobers! We're too curst to Heaven! You don't understand!

SMOKER: You can't doobers! We're too toast eleven! You don't stand under! You're not talking the same language any more!

WORKER: Borg?

SMOKER: *(Gesticulating)* You're not ... talking ... the same ... language ... any more!

WORKER: Glop?

SMOKER: You're not ... ohh ...

(More thunder. The SMOKER pulls down a plank. The thunder abruptly stops and the lights brighten. The WORKER grabs the plank and puts it back up: the thunder starts again and the lights dim. The SMOKER pulls it down: thunder stops, lights brighten. The WORKER, not experimenting, puts it up: thunder starts, lights dim. The WORKER, his eye on the sky, now slowly hands the plank to the SMOKER: thunder fades, sky fades up. The smoker continues dismantling in silence, while the WORKER looks on, bewildered. The sun is now bright, the sky peaceful. SMOKER glances up, sees the WORKER feeling useless and helpless, and silently offers him the cigarette he refused at the beginning of the play. Slowly the WORKER lights up and sits back, still trying to figure this thing out. The SMOKER works, the WORKER smokes. Gradually the WORKER's frown fades, and he is just beginning to relax and enjoy watching the birds when the lights slowly fade out)

BEING AT HOME WITH CLAUDE

by René-Daniel Dubois

Place: Judge Delorme's office in the Courthouse, Montreal
Time: 10:45 a.m., Monday, 4 July 1967
Characters: Him (Yves), the Inspector (Robert)

Him (Yves) is a male prostitute who, three days ago, cut the throat of one
of his regular johns. The victim was a young man named Claude, a
known separatist and a second-year literature student at the University of Montreal. After the murder, Yves waited for two days and then
tipped off the police as to the whereabouts of the body. An hour later,
he telephoned from Judge Delorme's office in the Courthouse (how
he got the keys nobody seems to know) to give himself up.

The Inspector does not want to create a public scandal while the 1967
World Exposition is going on in Montreal, and he refuses to let Yves
implicate Judge Delorme. After more than 30 hours of interrogation,
Yves and the Inspector are tired and frustrated. Yves is, at first,
hesitant but gradually reveals a history that is compelling and sad.

INSPECTOR: Do you still have a stomach ache?
HIM: It's almost gone.
INSPECTOR: Okay. So you ripped out the wires when you woke up?
HIM: No. I managed to go back to sleep. But it was the same kinda sleep
as before I woke up. Made me feel more exhausted than anything
else. I kept waking up, moaning.
INSPECTOR: Whaddaya mean?
HIM: I don't know how to describe it. I'd wake up and I couldn't tell
if I was awake or still asleep, or maybe I had been awake before and
now I was asleep. And my stomach ache was gettin' worse. At one

point I got up to piss. That's when I thought about the phone. I called his place.

INSPECTOR: Whose place?

HIM: HIS place.

INSPECTOR: Did you know his number by heart or did you have it written down somewhere?

HIM: There was no answer. Made me really mad, so I tore out the wire. As soon as I did it, I realized I didn't want to be there for anyone. Didn't want anyone to get in touch with me. Just wanted to disappear. Without even thinking, I went 'n' ripped out the doorbell. Wasn't very solid. I installed it myself when I moved in there. Then I unplugged the TV and the radio ... Then I went back to bed and I slept a little better.

INSPECTOR: Then what?

HIM: Then what? Nothing. I slept. I got up. I went back to bed. I slept. I woke up. I slept some more. 'Til Saturday evening.

INSPECTOR: What time Saturday?

HIM: I dunno. My clock had stopped. I forgot to wind it. I didn't even know what day it was and I couldn't've cared less.

INSPECTOR: But you looked at the clock cause you noticed it had stopped.

HIM: Yeah, but much later. Around 11 o'clock.

INSPECTOR: And you didn't leave the house at all between Friday morning and Saturday night?

HIM: No.

INSPECTOR: Didn't eat?

HIM: Maybe I ate something at my place.

INSPECTOR: Yesterday afternoon you told us you didn't mind eating sandwiches, you were used to it, you never eat at home, and when you don't have much money that's what you eat.

HIM: Yeah, but this time maybe I had somethin' in the house ...

INSPECTOR: Listen, don't start in again. Okay? There's nothing in your fridge, nothing in the garbage pail except dirty Kleenex, torn-up envelopes and some crumpled-up flyers, and ...

HIM: No. I didn't eat. And I wasn't hungry. I told you, I had a stomach ache.

INSPECTOR: Still no dope?

HIM: No.

INSPECTOR: What do you think made you sick?

HIM: I dunno.

INSPECTOR: Okay. So what happened at 11 o'clock?

HIM: I decided I'd had enough. That I had to get outta there. I took a shower and went out to get a couple of hot dogs. Then I came back and I called you. I called the reporter at home, but he had left. I called the newspaper. I told him my story. I came here. I let him and his photographer in and then I called you back.

INSPECTOR: You had his home number?

HIM: Yeah.

INSPECTOR: How did you get it?

HIM: You really think I'm gonna answer that question?

INSPECTOR: And you had his number at the paper too? He's not too shy, eh?

HIM: The phone book wasn't invented to wipe your ass with. I know how to read.

INSPECTOR: How come you don't want a lawyer?

HIM: I don't need one.

INSPECTOR: What makes you so sure the judge is gonna be able to bury this story? What makes you so sure he even wants to?

HIM: I never said he could ...

INSPECTOR: I know, I know. All you said was, you killed the guy on Casgrain. You wanted to turn yourself in but we had to come and get you here. And you wouldn't walk outta here 'til the judge agreed to meet you. The reporter is just here as a guarantee. That's all. And anyone who thinks that sounds like blackmail has a twisted mind ... right?

HIM: Why do you insist on puttin' all the pieces together? Somebody was killed. It's your job to find the murderer? You got him. What more do you want?

INSPECTOR: Are you as thick as you seem or have you decided to give me a hard time, just for the hell of it?

HIM: Just wait 'til the judge shows up, then we'll see ...

INSPECTOR: I've heard some weird stories in my time, but this one takes the cake. A guy turns himself in, even tho' the cops never could've found him cause no one ever would've connected him with the victim, but instead of keepin' his trap shut, he turns the fuckin' city upside down and blackmails a judge so the judge can find him innocent ... when he's the one who turned himself in.

HIM: You don't ...

INSPECTOR: And to top it all off ... he had no reason to kill the guy. He didn't take his money. He didn't take nothin'. He kills him then he goes downtown for a few drinks. At one point, he even considers going to check out the action on the mountain. Then he disappears and the next thing we know he's waiting for us at the Courthouse. And he gives us the runaround for 36 hours while we wait for the judge to show up. He doesn't want us to know his name. Doesn't want us to mention the name of the guy he killed. And he doesn't even want to tell us why. Holy Christ. And you're trying to tell me there's nothing wrong with you? Maybe I'm the one who's crazy? Give me a break. I'm supposed to leave on vacation tonight, not get fired ... Let's start all over again.

HIM: Oh, no. Not again.

INSPECTOR: Let's go.

HIM: Listen ...

INSPECTOR: I said: let's go. Left his place around ...

HIM: Nine o'clock.

INSPECTOR: Then what?

HIM: I took the metro to Bonaventure. Then I took a walk. I walked all the way to Westmount.

INSPECTOR: And from there?

HIM: I ran.

INSPECTOR: Where to?

HIM: Uuh ... to the Forum.

INSPECTOR: What did you wanta do at the Forum, in the middle of summer, at 10:30 at night on Confederation Day?

HIM: Make a phone call.

INSPECTOR: You trying to make me believe you ran all that way in the heat just for the thrill of using a phone at the Forum, when you must've passed about 40 phone booths during your little sprint?

HIM: Yes. No. I dunno. That's what I did. The way you tell it, it doesn't make any sense, but it made sense at the time.

INSPECTOR: You bet! ... Alright, so you finally reached the Forum?

HIM: Yeah, but it was locked up tight. I went over to the Alexis Nihon Plaza. I called his place. There was no answer. I thought I dialled the wrong number. I hung up and called back. No answer.

INSPECTOR: What's his number?

HIM: You know it as well as I do.

INSPECTOR: Tell me again.

HIM: Then I walked out onto Saint Catherine. The wind was gettin' stronger and there were lotsa people. Laughin' and havin' a good time. They were comin' out of the metro, wavin' little Canadian flags. I didn't feel like talking. I felt the way I feel when I come out of a good movie: the movie stays clear in my head until I start to talk about it. I know that if I talk about it, and I always do, I'm gonna lose the sense of it. But this wasn't even a good movie. It was a cop movie and the worst scene was stuck in my head. Anyway, I did what I always do, when I come out of the movies at Alexis Nihon Plaza, I headed east along Saint Catherine.

INSPECTOR: Okay. And while you were walking, before and after the phone call, did you hear anything? Did you notice any particular noises?

HIM: No.

INSPECTOR: You didn't hear any cannon shots?

HIM: This guy is a real pain. You keep askin' me the same fuckin' question and I keep givin' you the same fuckin' answer: No. I didn't hear any cannon shots. No jet planes. No bombs. No military parades. And I didn't find any grenades on the sidewalk.

INSPECTOR: Don't get wise. On the night of the first of July, there were fireworks on Saint Helen's Island. The people with the flags were coming back from there. You could hear them right up to Metropolitan Boulevard. So can you explain how you managed to take a walk along the harborfront without hearing them?

HIM: No ... I thought maybe he had gone out.We met at the Love Bar...

INSPECTOR: *(Shouts)* You don't say! It's about time! They met at the Love Bar. As simple as that. So you knew the guy?

HIM: Yes.

INSPECTOR: We're finally gettin' somewhere. When did you meet at the Love Bar? The day before the first of June?

HIM: ...

INSPECTOR: Are you the Yves he talks about in his diary?

HIM: ...

INSPECTOR: Great. Here we go again. He's pressed the Off button again. So you met at the Love Bar. Then what?

HIM: There's where we met. And I thought maybe he'd gone out. So I went to see if he was there. He wasn't. I checked out all the other bars. He wasn't there.

INSPECTOR: Did you meet anyone you know?

HIM: At least 40 people.

INSPECTOR: Where did you go afterwards?

HIM: To the Square. I'd told him ...

INSPECTOR: What? What did you tell him? When?

HIM: I'd told him I was gonna work that night.

INSPECTOR: When did you tell him that?

(Beat)

HIM: That afternoon, on the phone.

INSPECTOR: *(Relieved)* Phew.

HIM: Whatsa matter?

INSPECTOR: Nothing. Go on.

HIM: I told him there were so many tourists in town it was worth workin' two shifts a day. He didn't think it was very funny.

INSPECTOR: Why not?

HIM: Well ...

INSPECTOR: Was he jealous?

HIM: No. It was just a stupid joke, that's all.

INSPECTOR: Were you seeing each other regularly?

HIM: You should know. You said you read his diary.

INSPECTOR: Cut the shit and answer me ... Were you seeing each other regularly?

HIM: Yes.

INSPECTOR: You have a fight?

HIM: No.

INSPECTOR: So why did you kill him?

HIM: When he wasn't at home, I thought maybe he'd gone lookin' for me in the Square.

INSPECTOR: Had he ever gone looking for you in the Square?

HIM: No.

INSPECTOR: Why not? 'Cause he hated that scene?

HIM: No, no. You got it all wrong.

INSPECTOR: If you made more sense, maybe I wouldn't get so confused. What time was it when you arrived in the Square?

HIM: I was still around for the first last call at the Taureau ... I left right after ... Some guy, a customer, asked me where I was going. I told him. He said: Don't bother, how much? I took off anyway. He started after me, but he fell down the last seven or eight steps. Too pissed to hurt himself ... I dunno, the time it takes to walk there ... maybe it was 10 to three.

INSPECTOR: What were you thinking about?

HIM: I told you. I was thinkin' I must've missed him. We must've been in the wrong bars at the wrong times. And he'd come and meet me in the Square. I'd told him I was gonna be there.

INSPECTOR: You really thought he was still alive?

HIM: Yes. When I got there and saw everyone drinkin' and laughin', talkin' and cruisin', tokin' up and necking ... it kind of erased the picture. And I couldn't hear the ...
(He stops suddenly)

INSPECTOR: You couldn't hear what?
(Beat)

INSPECTOR: *(Louder)* What couldn't you hear?

HIM: There was quite a crowd in the Square ...

INSPECTOR: *(Interrupts him)* What couldn't you hear?

HIM: Huh?

INSPECTOR: Don't give me a hard time. You started to say something. You were saying that when you saw everyone in the bars having a good time, you couldn't hear ... you couldn't hear WHAT?

HIM: All I meant was, the music and seeing all those people made it seem impossible that he was gone. All those people who had been there the day before, and the day before that, and ever since I been going to those bars. Before I even knew him. Seemed impossible that they could still be around and him gone. Everything seemed too real. So the picture in my head was like ... erased.
(Pause)

INSPECTOR: *(Takes a deep breath, then)* What would you say if I told you your sister was waiting outside that door?
(Beat)

HIM: *(Stunned at first, then relaxes)* I'd laugh in your face.

INSPECTOR: Oh yeah?

HIM: It takes three days by car to get where she goes on vacation. And mountain climbers don't carry phones in their knapsacks.
(Beat)

INSPECTOR: Okay. So you had reached the Square.

HIM: You try to pull any other ones like that?

INSPECTOR: You reached the Square.

HIM: Hold on.

INSPECTOR: Too late. Should've thought of that earlier. The Square.

HIM: The bit about the diary ... was it true?

INSPECTOR: *(Goes to take a sip of the coffee he hasn't touched since he called his wife but it's cold)*

HIM: And the bit about his girlfriend?

INSPECTOR: Whatcha got against that girl?
(Beat)

INSPECTOR: Let's get on with it. You reached the Square. What time did you get there?

HIM: I told you five minutes ago. The time it took to hear the first last call at the Taureau, go out the door, down the stairs and walk over to the Square.

INSPECTOR: You didn't stop anywhere on the way?

HIM: No.

INSPECTOR: Didn't meet anyone you knew?

HIM: No.

INSPECTOR: Okay. So you reached the Square. Then what?

HIM: I sat down on a bench, over by the caleches.

INSPECTOR: In the park?

HIM: Yeah. Along the walk that leads to Peel.

INSPECTOR: The first bench on the walk?

HIM: Yeah.

INSPECTOR: How come your friends didn't see you?

HIM: Who says my friends didn't see me? Maybe that's another one of your stories ...

INSPECTOR: If you had talked to your friends, you'd know I was lying. I could only be making it up if you didn't talk to them. Are you sure you went to the Square?

HIM: Yes.

INSPECTOR: So how come your friends didn't see you?

HIM: 'Cause I usually move around. And I hang out around the statue.

INSPECTOR: How come you didn't go there this time?

HIM: I didn't feel like it.

INSPECTOR: Why didn't you feel like it?

HIM: 'Cause I felt like bein' alone. That's why.

INSPECTOR: So why did you go to the Square?

HIM: 'Cause I didn't feel like stayin' at the Taureau for the parade, and I felt ...

INSPECTOR: Parade? What parade?

HIM: The game. When everyone knows the last call is comin' up, they go to the john and comb their hair, splash some water on their face and then they line up as close to the door as possible, so they can't miss anyone who's leavin' on his own. I call it the parade. I didn't feel like watchin' it that night and I didn't feel like goin' home either. I wasn't sleepy. So I went over to the Square before everyone else and I didn't go to my usual spot. That's why nobody saw me. I was sittin' on a bench facing Peel.

INSPECTOR: For how long?

HIM: Not long.

INSPECTOR: You sure?

HIM: Yeah, 'cause I left before the whole gang started to arrive.

INSPECTOR: How long?

HIM: The time it takes to walk outta Pepe's and cross half the park, lengthwise.

INSPECTOR: Huh?

HIM: I'd just sat down when I heard someone shouting in the middle of Peel Street. I stood up. At first I thought someone got hit by a car ... but it was just a bunch of Americans comin' outta Pepe's. Having a good time. They stopped the traffic to cross Peel and they came into the park 'n' went over to take a look at the statue. Then they headed towards me.

INSPECTOR: To talk to you?

HIM: No. They wanted to go for a caleche ride. I'd sat back down on the back of the bench. They walked right by me. There was one good-lookin' one in the gang but he was the drunkest. They all looked at me when they walked by. The good-lookin' one stopped and gave me a big smile ... then he went and caught up with the others. They were talking with one of the caleche drivers. Then they went over to another one. None of the drivers wanted to take them cause they all wanted to go in the same caleche and they were too pissed. All of a sudden the good-lookin' guy covered his face with his hands for a second, then looked up at the sky. Then he turned around slowly and he saw me. Another big grin. And he came over and sat down beside me. On the seat of the bench, not on the back. He muttered something. I think he was apologizing for being too drunk to keep his balance on the back of the bench. Then he asked me to get down 'n' sit beside him. So I did. He asked me if I wanted to go home with him. I told him it would cost him. He asked me how much. I told him and he gave it to me right away. He put his hand on my neck to get me to stand up. He shouted "bye" to his friends and we headed towards Peel to grab a cab. His friends shouted something at him. We took a cab to the corner of Pine and Aylmer. It had started to rain. He was staying in a flat there with his friends. It belonged to one of them who's studying at McGill. He said we'd have plenty of time before they got back. But he didn't touch me. Usually I can't stand customers who beat around the bush. I like it short and sweet. Don't like hangin' around for an hour waiting for something to happen. But he didn't touch me and I didn't mind. He took out a map of the city and started askin' me different things. Where was the Wax Museum, stuff like that. I told him. He was really pissed and he started to make a speech. Couldn't understand much of it, but I think he was talking about one-night stands and people who hang out in bars checking each other out for hours, without ever saying a word. People who don't wanta talk, they just wanta fuck. He seemed fed up. Then he finally said, alright, let's go to bed. We went into the bedroom, he threw himself on the bed and fell asleep on the spot. I undressed him tucked him in. He was sound asleep. I looked at him lying there sleeping. Then I turned out the lights and left ... *(Beat)* ... I left his money on the table ... *(Beat)* First time I ever did that. I always figured, once they get me there, what the fuck do I care if anything happens or not. Like at the dentist's. You got an appointment. They charge you whether you come or not. But this time, it just didn't seem ... Something ... When I got outside, it had almost stopped raining. I walked back to the Square. I knew there was something waiting for me there. I didn't know what. But I had to go see ... Anyway, it was there in the bedroom with the surfer ... that I realized that I wasn't gonna be anyone's chicken anymore.

INSPECTOR: ...

HIM: It's got nothing to do with how old you are. Chicken is a way of life. A way of looking at life. It means going through life with a little smirk on your face, a smirk that says everything's gonna be fine, even if you're up to your eyebrows in shit. A smirk most people don't even notice. When it works, you stretch out naked on the bearskin rug and strut your stuff. And when it doesn't, you take off, on your tiptoes, the way you sneak away from some customer's house, at five in the morning while he's sound asleep. Saying to yourself, that guy was really cheap, but there'll be others. And you take off with his watch if you feel like he took more than he gave.

(Pause)

INSPECTOR: Finished?

HIM: *(He nods yes)*

INSPECTOR: My turn now. Now that you've told me everything that crossed your mind. I'm surprised we didn't get to hear about your ancestors and when they first arrived from Brittany. And I still don't know any more than I did at one o'clock yesterday morning. You want me to tell you what I think of your story? Eh? Want me to tell you what I think you're after?

HIM: *(Doesn't budge)*

INSPECTOR: Stop looking at me like I was dogshit. I wasn't born wearing a uniform. But I'm not about to tell you my life story just to make you cry. Your friend there ... Thursday night ... when you went to see him, I think you were stoned. Stoned outta your mind. I think you got into a fight 'cause he lives on Casgrain while you work the Square for money, and the mountain for fun. I think you got into a fight and you lost control. I think you went nuts 'cause he wanted to kick you out. I think you killed him without realizing what you were doing. Then you went home and hid. And when you came down off your high, you were scared shitless. And you made up this whole friggin' story, just hoping you could pass for crazy. Right? Called the reporters. Arranged to steal Judge Delorme's keys. Where did you get them? Huh? Forget it. Don't bother. I know. In his pants pocket. Perfect set-up for blackmail, right? Did you steal them before you killed your boyfriend or after?

HIM: After.

INSPECTOR: That's right. What could he do about it? If he calls the cops, he's cooked, right? And all you had to do is call him and tell him: keep this case outta the papers or I call the reporters, or your wife, or the provincial police and I show them the keys ... Am I right or not?

HIM: No.

INSPECTOR: No? No, what? When are you gonna come out with it, for the love of Christ? Why did you take them? And when did you change your mind? And why? Listen. I've met hundreds of smartass kids like you. Ten a day, every day, for the past five years. I've seen all kinds. Some get into it 'cause they need the money to pay for university, and when they've got enough money, they stop. Some of them start one night when they're high on acid and they never come down. Others it's just too much beer. Some of them do it 'cause they're starving to death. Some come down from Outremont, just for the trip. They come in all shapes and sizes. Tall and short, fat or skinny as a toothpick. I've seen some with faces that look like they been carved with a tomahawk. And others with real babyfaces. It's the 50-year-old ones that scare the shit outta you. Sometimes I wake up in a cold sweat in the middle of the night, thinking I can smell their perfume ... I'm not stupid. I know chickens aren't just something you eat for Sunday dinner. I knew it before you were even born. And your profound observations on the subject aren't teaching me a thing. Nothing! So drop the pretty speeches and deliver the goods.

HIM: (*Stares at the INSPECTOR without blinking. Makes no move to respond. Pause*)

INSPECTOR: Okay. So let me tell you something else. Something you can call my wife and tell her when you get outta jail, or if they give you one last wish. Something I've never told anyone. There are times

when I'm sitting at my desk and they're sitting there across from me and I look at them and I feel like crying my eyes out. Sometimes, if Guy wasn't there to transcribe what they're saying, I wouldn't be able to remember what they said for two, three, maybe 10 minutes. I don't hear a thing. Nothing. They could be speaking Hebrew or Arabic, for all I understand. And it takes every last bit of strength I got not to tell Guy to leave. Not to get up and go over to them and take them in my arms. Okay? *(Beat)* I've seen all kinds. You name it. But I hope I'll never see another one like you as long as I fuckin' live. I hope you're the only one of your kind. 'Cause your little trip is the lousiest, the sickest trip I've ever seen.
(Pause)

INSPECTOR: *(Slowly, deliberately)* I don't know how I'm gonna prevent you from getting what you want. But you can be sure, I'm gonna do everything I can. I dunno how I'm gonna prove you stole those keys. I dunno know if I'm gonna have to commit perjury, but I'm gonna prevent you from implicating the judge. Not because he's a buddy. Not because there's anything in it for me. Not even to save my job; I've had tougher nuts to crack. I'm gonna do it just for the pleasure of shutting you up and taking you out of circulation. And for that pleasure, I'm willing to do anything. You hear me? Anything. I'm gonna get you. You can count on it. *(Beat)* And for starters, I got a big disappointment for you. Your reporter friends aren't even gonna get to see you walk outta here.

BLOOD RELATIONS

Sharon Pollock

Place: the Borden House; Fall River, Massachusetts
Time: late Sunday afternoon, late autumn, in 1902
Characters: Miss Lizzie, the Actress

Ten years after she allegedly killed her father and her stepmother with
an ax, Lizzie Borden is still living in the old Borden house. She and
her actress-friend, who has come from Boston to stay, are the stuff
of gossip in Fall River now. The townsfolk are suspicious about their
relationship and, as Lizzie's sister Emma maintains, Lizzie "should do
nothing to inspire talk," having recently been acquitted of murder.

The Actress is intrigued by the possibility that Lizzie has, indeed,
committed the murders. There are several reasons why she might
have: she hated her stepmother; her father was a rigid old patriarch,
and Lizzie was apparently being written out of his will. The Actress is
obsessed with finding out the truth and regularly asks Lizzie to "paint
the background again," hoping she will give something away.

Lights up on the figure of a woman standing center stage. It is a somewhat
formal pose. A pause. She speaks:
"Since what I am about to say must be but that
Which contradicts my accusation, and
The testimony on my part no other
But what comes from myself, it shall scarce boot me
To say 'Not Guilty.'
But, if Powers Divine
Behold our human action as they do,
I doubt not than but innocence shall make
False accusation blush and tyranny
Tremble at ... at ..."
(She wriggles the fingers of an outstretched hand searching for the word)
"Aaaat" ... Bollocks!!

(She raises her script, takes a bit of chocolate)
"Tremble at Patience," patience patience! ...
(MISS LIZZIE enters from the kitchen with tea service. THE ACTRESS's attention drifts to MISS LIZZIE. THE ACTRESS watches MISS LIZZIE sit in the parlor and proceed to pour two cups of tea. THE ACTRESS sucks her teeth a bit to clear the chocolate as she speaks)

THE ACTRESS: Which ... is proper, Lizzie?

MISS LIZZIE: Proper?

THE ACTRESS: To pour first the cream, and add the tea - or first tea and add cream. One is proper. Is the way you do the proper way, the way it's done in circles where it counts?

MISS LIZZIE: Sugar?

THE ACTRESS: Well, is it?

MISS LIZZIE: I don't know, sugar?

THE ACTRESS: Mmmm. *(MISS LIZZIE adds sugar)* I suppose if we had Mrs. Beeton's *Book of Etiquette*, we could look it up.

MISS LIZZIE: I do have it, shall I get it?

THE ACTRESS: No ... You could ask your sister, she might know.

MISS LIZZIE: Do you want this tea or not?

THE ACTRESS: I hate tea.

MISS LIZZIE: You drink it every Sunday.

THE ACTRESS: I drink it because you like to serve it.

MISS LIZZIE: Pppu.

THE ACTRESS: It's true. You've no idea how I suffer from this toast and tea ritual. I really do. The tea upsets my stomach and the toast makes me fat because I eat so much of it.

MISS LIZZIE: Practise some restraint then.

THE ACTRESS: Mmmmm ... Why don't we ask you sister which is proper?

MISS LIZZIE: You ask her.

THE ACTRESS: How can I? She doesn't speak to me. I don't think she even sees me. She gives no indication of it. *(She looks up the stairs)* What do you suppose she does up there every Sunday afternoon?

MISS LIZZIE: She sulks.

THE ACTRESS: And reads the Bible I suppose, and Mrs. Beeton's *Book of Etiquette*. Oh Lizzie ... What a long day. The absolutely longest day ... When does that come anyway, the longest day?

MISS LIZZIE: June.

THE ACTRESS: Ah yes, June. *(She looks at MISS LIZZIE)* June?

MISS LIZZIE: June.

THE ACTRESS: Mmmmmm ...

MISS LIZZIE: I know what you're thinking.

THE ACTRESS: Of course you do ... I'm thinking ... shall I pour the sherry - or will you.

MISS LIZZIE: No.

THE ACTRESS: I'm thinking ... June ... in Fall River.

MISS LIZZIE: No.

THE ACTRESS: August in Fall River? *(She smiles. Pause)*

MISS LIZZIE: We could have met in Boston.

THE ACTRESS: I prefer it here.

MISS LIZZIE: You don't find it ... a trifle boring?

THE ACTRESS: Au contraire.

(MISS LIZZIE gives a small laugh at the affectation)

THE ACTRESS: What?

MISS LIZZIE: I find it a trifle boring ... I know what you're doing. You're soaking up the ambience.

THE ACTRESS: Nonsense, Lizzie. I come to see you.

MISS LIZZIE: Why?

THE ACTRESS: Because ... of us. *(Pause)*

MISS LIZZIE: You were a late arrival last night. Later than usual.

THE ACTRESS: Don't be silly.

MISS LIZZIE: I wonder why.

THE ACTRESS: The show was late, late starting, late coming down.

MISS LIZZIE: And?

THE ACTRESS: And - then we all went out for drinks.

MISS LIZZIE: We?

THE ACTRESS: The other members of the cast.

MISS LIZZIE: Oh yes.

THE ACTRESS: And then I caught a cab ... all the way from Boston ... Do you know what it cost?

MISS LIZZIE: I should. I paid the bill, remember?

THE ACTRESS: *(Laughs)* Of course. What a jumble all my thoughts are. There're too many words running round inside my head today. It's terrible.

MISS LIZZIE: It sounds it.

(Pause)

THE ACTRESS: ... You know ... you do this thing ... you stare at me ... You look directly at my eyes. I think ... you think ... that if I'm lying ... it will come up, like lemons on a slot machine. *(She makes a gesture at her eyes)* Tick. Tick ... *(Pause)* In the alley, behind the theater the other day, there were some kids. You know what they were doing?

MISS LIZZIE: How could I?

THE ACTRESS: They were playing skip rope, and you know what they were singing?

(She sings, and claps her hands arhythmically to:)

"Lizzie Borden took an ax

Gave her mother 40 whacks,

When the job was nicely done,

She gave her father 41."

MISS LIZZIE: Did you stop them?

THE ACTRESS: No.

MISS LIZZIE: Did you tell them I was acquitted?

THE ACTRESS: No.

MISS LIZZIE: What did you do?

THE ACTRESS: I shut the window.

MISS LIZZIE: A noble gesture on my behalf.

THE ACTRESS: We were doing lines - the noise they make is dreadful. Sometimes they play ball, ka-thunk, ka-thunk, ka-thunk against the wall. Once I saw them with a cat and -

MISS LIZZIE: And you didn't stop them?

THE ACTRESS: That time I stopped them.

(THE ACTRESS crosses to table where there is a gramophone. She prepares to play a record. She stops)

THE ACTRESS: Should I?

MISS LIZZIE: Why not?

THE ACTRESS: Your sister, the noise upsets her.

MISS LIZZIE: And she upsets me. On numerous occasions.

THE ACTRESS: You're incorrigible, Lizzie.

(THE ACTRESS holds out her arms to MISS LIZZIE. They dance the latest "in" dance, a Scott Joplin composition. It requires some concentration, but they chat while dancing rather formally in contrast to the music)

THE ACTRESS: ... Do you think your jawline's heavy?

MISS LIZZIE: Why do you ask?

THE ACTRESS: They said you had jowls.

MISS LIZZIE: Did they.

THE ACTRESS: The reports of the day said you were definitely jowly.

MISS LIZZIE: That was 10 years ago.

THE ACTRESS: Imagine. You were only 34.

MISS LIZZIE: Yes.

THE ACTRESS: It happened here, this house.

MISS LIZZIE: You're leading.

THE ACTRESS: I know.

MISS LIZZIE: ... I don't think I'm jowly. Then or now. Do you?

THE ACTRESS: Lizzie? Lizzie.

MISS LIZZIE: What?

THE ACTRESS: ... did you?

MISS LIZZIE: Did I what?

(Pause)

THE ACTRESS: You never tell ME anything. *(She turns off the music)*

MISS LIZZIE: I tell you everything.

THE ACTRESS: No you don't!

MISS LIZZIE: Oh yes, I tell you the most personal things about myself, my thoughts, my dreams, my -

THE ACTRESS: But never that one thing ... *(She lights a cigarette)*

MISS LIZZIE: And don't smoke those - they stink.

(THE ACTRESS ignores her, inhales, exhales a volume of smoke in MISS LIZZIE's direction)

MISS LIZZIE: Do you suppose ... people buy you drinks ... or cast you even ... because you have a "liaison" with Lizzie Borden? Do you suppose they do that?

THE ACTRESS: They cast me because I'm good at what I do.

MISS LIZZIE: They never pry? They never ask? What's she really like? Is she really jowly? Did she? Didn't she?

THE ACTRESS: What could I tell them? You never tell me anything.

MISS LIZZIE: I tell you everything.

THE ACTRESS: But that! *(Pause)* You think everybody talks about you - they don't.

MISS LIZZIE: Here they do.

THE ACTRESS: You think they talk about you.

MISS LIZZIE: But never to me.

THE ACTRESS: Well ... you give them lots to talk about.

MISS LIZZIE: You know you're right, your mind is a jumble.

THE ACTRESS: I told you so.

(Pause)

MISS LIZZIE: You remind me of my sister.

THE ACTRESS: Oh God, in what way?

MISS LIZZIE: Day in, day out, 10 years now, sometimes at breakfast as she rolls little crumbs of bread in little balls, sometimes at noon, or late at night ... "Did you, Lizzie?" "Lizzie, did you?"

THE ACTRESS: Ten years, day in, day out?

MISS LIZZIE: Oh yes. She sits there where Papa used to sit and I sit there, where I have always sat. She looks at me and at her plate, then at me, and at her plate, then at me and then she says "Did you, Lizzie?" "Lizzie, did you?"

THE ACTRESS: *(A nasal imitation of Emma's voice)* "Did-you-Lizzie - Lizzie-did-you." *(Laughs)*

MISS LIZZIE: Did I what?

THE ACTRESS: *(Continues her imitation of Emma)* "You know."

MISS LIZZIE: Well, what do you think?

THE ACTRESS: "Oh, I believe you didn't, in fact I know you didn't, what a thought! After all, you were acquitted."

MISS LIZZIE: Yes, I was.

THE ACTRESS: "But sometimes when I'm on the street ... or shopping ... or at the church even, I catch somebody's eye, they look away ... and I think to myself "Did-you-Lizzie - Lizzie-did-you."

MISS LIZZIE: *(Laughs)* Ah, poor Emma.

THE ACTRESS: *(Dropping her Emma imitation)* Well, did you?

MISS LIZZIE: Is it important?

THE ACTRESS: Yes.

MISS LIZZIE: Why?

THE ACTRESS: I have ... a compulsion to know the truth.

MISS LIZZIE: The truth?

THE ACTRESS: Yes.

MISS LIZZIE: ... Sometimes I think you look like me, and you're not jowly.

THE ACTRESS: No.

MISS LIZZIE: You look like me, or how I think I look, or how I ought to look ... sometimes you think like me ... do you feel that?

THE ACTRESS: Sometimes.

MISS LIZZIE: *(Triumphant)* You shouldn't have to ask then. You should know. "Did I, didn't I." You tell me.

THE ACTRESS: I'll tell you what I think ... I think ... that you're aware there is a certain fascination in the ambiguity ... You always paint the background but leave the rest to my imagination. Did Lizzie Borden take an ax? ... If you didn't I should be disappointed ... and if you did I should be horrified.

THE BOX
Sheldon Rosen

Place: apartment of Man One and Man Two
Time: around suppertime on a Tuesday; year unspecified; the play was first produced in 1974
Characters: Man One, Man Two

At the beginning of Sheldon Rosen's very theatrical one-act The Box, Man Two is discovered, sitting in a chair and reading a newspaper. He makes a living by cutting out newspaper clippings and sending them to people. Man One enters with excessive gusto, an energy created, perhaps, by his expectations concerning a gift-wrapped box which he will open by the end of the play. The box has a card attached, apparently addressed to Man One, which reads: "To my dearest nephew. A little remembrance from a fellow dreamer. Something you've always wanted. Love forever and ever. Aunt Silly." Man One has wanted roller skates since he was 11 years old; he would be crushed, he says, if the box did not contain roller skates.

TWO: Aren't you just the slightest bit curious?
ONE: Curiosity killed the cat.
TWO: *(Exasperated)* Oh wow! Look, why don't you just open it up and get it over with?
ONE: It's easy for you, but what happens to me if it isn't roller skates?
TWO: So it's not roller skates, big deal.
ONE: Maybe not for you, but I've been wanting roller skates since I was 11.
TWO: What makes you think there's skates in the box?
ONE: *(He takes the box and reads a card attached to it)* "To my dearest nephew. A little remembrance from a fellow dreamer. Something you've always wanted. Love forever and ever. Aunt Silly." She loved me very much. So there. She always gave me money and mocha bars.
TWO: So that means there's roller skates in the box?
ONE: Maybe. If I opened the box and there weren't roller skates inside, I would cry forever and my cheeks would wrinkle and shrivel up and I would become an old man before my time.
TWO: You really want skates, don't you?
ONE: More than anything.

TWO: Why?

ONE: Why? What difference does it make? ... I don't remember exactly anymore. But I do want them.

TWO: If you didn't want roller skates so badly, would you open up the box?

ONE: Sure. There might be something we could use inside. I sometimes sincerely wish that I didn't want rink roller skates.

TWO: Do you mean that?

ONE: I think so.

TWO: I can make you not want skates, you know.

ONE: You can?

TWO: Sure. Sometimes I read in the weekend magazine section of the paper. I just have to strap you into the chair. Sit over here.
(The chair is facing the audience)

ONE: What for?

TWO: So you won't want roller skates.

ONE: I don't know how you're going to make me forget roller skates by tying me up with your belt.

TWO: You'll see.

ONE: Your pants are falling.

TWO: Forget my pants and sit still.

ONE: *(While he is being tied in the chair)* Are you going to ask me about my relatives now?

TWO: There.
(He is finished)

ONE: *(Laughing)* You look silly. I can't help it.
(MAN TWO squirts him)

ONE: Ahhh ... what the hell was that?

TWO: Lemon juice.

ONE: Well, you squirted me right in the eyes. What did you do that for?

TWO: You'll see. *(He clicks a clicker)* What do you see on the screen?

ONE: A pair of terrific-looking rink roller skates.
(Squirt)

ONE: Owww! Hey, now cut that out!

TWO: Open your eyes and tell me again what you see ... slowly.

ONE: I see ...

TWO: Yes.

ONE: A ...

TWO: Uh huh.

ONE: ... pair of ...

TWO: Yeah.

ONE: ... terrific-looking ...
(Squirt)

ONE: Oww!

TWO: Open your eyes.

ONE: No!

(Sound of a striking match)

ONE: Ow, goddamnit, you're burning my eyelashes. You crazy or something?

TWO: It's for your own good. Now open your eyes and start again. What do you see?

ONE: A pair of ...

TWO: Yes. *(Pause)* Yes.

ONE: I don't think I want to say anymore.

TWO: Why not?

ONE: I'm a little scared.

TWO: Go ahead. There's nothing to be afraid of ... say it.

ONE: A pair of ...

TWO: Yes.

ONE: *(Quickly)* ... terrific-looking ...

(Squirt)

ONE: Oww. I knew you were going to do it.

TWO: Again!

ONE: I see a pair of ... *(Pause)* ... roller skates? *(Pause)* A pair of roller skates. I see a pair of roller skates.

TWO: Good. *(Click)* And now.

ONE: Oh wow! That's me having fun on a pair of roller skates.

TWO: What?

ONE: That's me having fun -

(Squirts)

 ONE: Oww! That's me on roller skates.

TWO: Very good. *(Click)* And now?

ONE: Ooo! I'm on roller skates at the top of a hill.

TWO: How do you feel?

ONE: Hesitant. A little nervous, excited.

TWO: Can you see over the edge?

ONE: I have to stretch to see. I don't want to lose my balance.

TWO: *(The click and then exertion, as if he has pushed MAN ONE)* And now.

ONE: Aw, someone pushed me.

(Click)

ONE: I'm going down the hill.

(Click)

ONE: Faster and faster. Too fast.

(Click)

ONE: Much too fast!

(Click)

ONE: There's a bridge ahead.

(Click)

ONE: Too narrow.

(Click)

ONE: I can't stop. Still getting faster. I can't use my arms!

(Click)

ONE: I can't look down. The water's so deep. Can't look down.

(Click)

ONE: I'm sick. Oh god, I'm so sick.

(Click)

ONE: My arms won't move. I can't stop. On the bridge and still going faster.

(Click)

ONE: The bridge isn't finished!

(Click)

ONE: I can't stop.

(Click)

ONE: I'm going off the edge.

(Click)

ONE: Agghhh!

(Pause)

TWO: Are you all right?

ONE: Oh god. I thought I was going off the edge.

TWO: A dream?

ONE: I was sick to my stomach.

TWO: A bad dream.

ONE: My feet were so heavy. They had wheels. Roller skates. I couldn't get them off. Like cement. Couldn't get them off.

TWO: Sounds awful.

ONE: It was awful.

TWO: You're shaking.

ONE: I'm soaking wet - I can't move my arms!

TWO: I'll get you a blanket.

ONE: So cold.

TWO: There you go. Let me unstrap your arms.

ONE: Why am I strapped up?

TWO: I had to do it for your own good.

ONE: Bad dream ...

TWO: I have something for you.

ONE: A surprise?

TWO: How did you know?

ONE: I can move my arms now.

TWO: It's for you.

(He hands MAN ONE the box)

ONE: What a pretty ribbon.

TWO: Aren't you going to open it?

ONE: Now?

TWO: Of course.

ONE: Of course, now I remember. I was drowning. The water was filling my nose and choking my lungs and my feet were carrying me deeper and darker, but somehow I managed to find me a comfortable position and I looked up and saw me opening a box with a pretty red ribbon and soft, blue tissue paper. I untied the ribbon very carefully and put it in a drawer. Then I slowly unpeeled the cello tape holding the tissue paper together and gently pushed the paper aside. There was a cardboard packing box inside. It said, "Chiquita Brand Banana" on it. The box was held shut by adhesive tape. I remember being surprised by how white the tape still was. I started pulling the tape off. It ripped the outer skin of the box. It was an uncomfortable sound. I had a little trouble breathing. I took three complete breaths. *(He does now)* And lifted the flaps of the box. There was more tissue paper inside. It was easy to get through. And there it was.

TWO: What! Tell me what!

ONE: What difference does it make?

TWO: Whattaya mean, what difference does it make?

ONE: Such a lovely red ribbon.

TWO: Open it, goddamn you!

ONE: Oh yes, I remember now. I looked up and saw you standing over me. You took the box away from me.

TWO: Give me that box, you moron.

ONE: You pulled off the ribbon and ripped the tissue paper and broke your nail trying to get the tape off.

TWO: Ow, goddamnit!

ONE: You tore the box open and found a pair of wings inside.

TWO: Wings inside? *(He stops unwrapping the box)* Wings in a box?

ONE: Very carefully folded. You nearly ripped them pulling them out.

TWO: I better be careful.

ONE: They were lovely. You had to unfold them. The spun fiber was very soft, but strong. You must have had a span of a good six feet or more. They were folded in quarters. You held them up. They shone copper and orange and blue in the sun. They had long, sharp, curved hooks attached to them that penetrated your flesh and locked onto your bone. I helped you adjust them. They hooked on at the shoulder blade and lower rib cage. Copper bands fit over your arms. There was blood rolling down your back and splashing onto the floor. Wet, red scales of blood. The room was too small for you. You squeezed yourself out through the window and into the ledge. You told me not to push you.

TWO: I'll go when I'm ready.

ONE: You didn't jump, you just slowly let your arms rise and fall.
(MAN TWO begins to do so. It almost becomes a dance as MAN TWO explores the different possible wing movements)

ONE: Rising and falling. Rising and falling. Rise, fall, rise, fall ... rising ... and faallling ....

(MAN TWO continues to move)

ONE: I watched the muscles in your arms and shoulders come together and stretch apart. Such beautiful, strong, smooth, sinewy muscles. Then slowly you rose off the ledge and glided away. Faster and faster. I didn't even know where you were going.

TWO: *(Arms outstretched as if gliding - no flapping)* To the sea.

ONE: Oh, that's right.

TWO: That's beautiful.

ONE: Yes, it was. You seemed so happy. I really was pleased for you.

TWO: *(Notices MAN ONE staring at his outstretched arms. He self-consciously brings them down)* Were you?

ONE: Of course I was. *(Pause)* Aren't you going to open it?

TWO: I said, "Don't push." I said, "I'll go when I'm ready."

ONE: *(Shaking the box)* Definitely wings in here. They sure would come in handy. You could always use a good pair of wings. You got lots of places you want to see. Lots of beaches.

TWO: *(He has been staring intently at MAN ONE. He feels himself being manipulated. He breaks off the stare and sits back down in the chair, picks up the newspaper and begins reading again. After a bit he laughs to himself)* Wings in a box. The oldest trick in the book. You must think I'm as dumb as you look.

ONE: Trick! Who keeps pestering me with roller skates? Who told me about an ocean in a box and swimming and who pushed me off the top of the hill, eh? Who did that? I'm talking to you, goddamnit! WHO?

TWO: *(He delivers all his lines from behind his newspaper)* Was that you who-ing? I thought there was an owl in the room.

ONE: Open your box.

TWO: *(Quietly)* Fuck off.

ONE: *(Knocks roughly at the paper)* Come out and open your box.

TWO: I'm busy.

ONE: I'll smash it.

TWO: It's your box. It's always been your box.

ONE: No it isn't. It's your box. *(He takes the box and changes the wording on the card)* "To my dearest friend. A little remembrance from a fellow dreamer. Something you've always wanted. Love forever and ever. me." You hear me? This one is yours.

(MAN TWO does not answer. He just turns another page of his newspaper. MAN ONE picks up the box and smashes it through the paper and onto MAN TWO's lap. MAN TWO takes the box and places it on the floor at his feet. MAN ONE goes to the cupboard and gets a hammer. He is still playing. MAN TWO puts down his paper and watches. MAN ONE gently taps the box with the hammer. Then a little harder. Goaded on by MAN TWO watching, MAN ONE goes berserk and attacks the box, smashing it right in front of MAN TWO. MAN TWO is very deliberately under control at this point. MAN ONE is shredding the box with hands. A pair of badly

mangled roller skates falls out. MAN ONE screams. He picks up the skates as if they were a dead baby. He is on his knees, crying softly, in front of MAN TWO. There is a long pause as MAN TWO stares out into the audience. Finally MAN TWO rises from the chair and begins to clean up the mess. He gathers everything into a pile. He takes the skates from MAN ONE. He looks at them.)

TWO: They're only size five. They would have been too small.

COLD COMFORT

Jim Garrard

Place: "the former office/showroom of a rundown service station located just off the trans-Canada highway not far from Gull Lake, Saskatchewan"; the room is now used as a living accomodation by Floyd and his daughter Dolores.

Time: 10:00 p.m., a weekday night, late March, early 1980s

Characters: Floyd, now in his late 40s or early 50s; his daughter Dolores, 15; Stephen

Floyd and his daughter Dolores have emigrated to Saskatchewan from the badlands of Alberta. Dolores' mother did not come with them; Floyd "never talks about her anymore." Dolores is very attached to her father, even though he is capable of unequivocally nasty misdoings. When she was eight, Dolores says, her father tied her down to the workbench, chloroformed her and, in a fit of rage, operated on her abdomen, removing some of her insides.

Stephen, a marketing representative with an international jewelry company, has been stranded by a spring blizzard on a sideroad a few miles from the garage. Floyd, in his towtruck, has found Stephen's car (still running; Stephen was inside but almost dead from carbon monoxide poisoning) and has towed it back to the garage.

There he "gives" Stephen to Dolores as a present because she has been complaining about her loneliness. Floyd then retires to the adjoining shop, on the pretense that he has work to do. Stephen soon revives and, after some questions and answers, treats Dolores to an exquisite lunch that he had packed in his cooler for the long trip from Regina to Calgary. Dolores announces that she needs a bath, hauls in a portable tub, and proceeds to bathe in full view of Stephen. She finishes her bath and slips into her pyjamas and a bathrobe, moments before the following scene begins.

DOLORES: How about another glass of wine?
(He fills her glass without speaking)
A bath makes you feel so good. Especially with that foamy stuff.
STEPHEN: You look terrific.
DOLORES: What kind of wine is this?
STEPHEN: It's German.
DOLORES: Does it have a name?
STEPHEN: I hate to say it really. Liebfraumilch.
DOLORES: What did you do today?
STEPHEN: *(Laughing)* I got stuck in a snowbank.
DOLORES: No. Before that.
STEPHEN: This morning, I drove to Regina. This afternoon, I had a meeting with a tool manufacturer.
DOLORES: Did you sell him anything?
STEPHEN: I did, as a matter of fact.
DOLORES: Are you a good salesman?
STEPHEN: I think so.
(Beat)
How old are you?
DOLORES: Eighteen.
(Beat)
Well, 17, really. I'll be 18 on Monday. *(She hears a sound)*
DOLORES: Here he is. It's him. Daddy's coming back.
(We hear a truck outside. She hurries out through the service bay door, closing it. We hear the door roll up and the truck drive into the service bay. The door rolls down and we hear FLOYD getting out of the truck. The door opens and he comes in, followed by DOLORES. He goes straight for the space heater and warms himself)
FLOYD: Well, young fellow, how are you making out?
DOLORES: We're having a party, Daddy. Sort of. Look at all this stuff. I had a bubble bath and Stephen gave me some German wine. Didn't you, Stephen?
STEPHEN: Would you care for a glass yourself, sir?
FLOYD: I think I need a whiskey.
(She gets it for him immediately, taking his coat and hanging it up. He sits in the armchair and removes his boots. She brings him his slippers and begins to rub the stiffness out of his shoulders and his upper back. He studies STEPHEN)
So you're getting my little girl all liquored up.
STEPHEN: It's just a light wine. I hope you don't mind. *(He lights a small cigar)*
FLOYD: Christ, why should I mind? If she's happy, I'm happy. Get me my tobacco out of that coat you took away, will you, honey? *(She gets him his tobacco)*
STEPHEN: Would you care for a cigar? They're very good.

FLOYD: No, I'll stick to what I'm used to, thanks.
(All three sit in silence)
(STEPHEN and FLOYD smoke)
STEPHEN: *(Finally)* Any break in the weather?
FLOYD: Never mind about the goddamn weather. What I want to know is whether you been up on her yet or not?
DOLORES: Daddy!
FLOYD: Well, have you or haven't you?
STEPHEN: I'm not sure what you mean.
FLOYD: Don't play the dumb ass with me. Did you screw this girl while I was gone out of here, or didn't you?
(DOLORES flies at FLOYD in great distress. She lands on him full force and beats his shoulders and chest with clenched fists)
DOLORES: Don't be so mean. Don't you be so mean. You don't have to embarrass me just when I'm having a nice time for a change. You're just too mean. You're crude and vulgar and dirty and mean. *(He subdues her by wrapping his arms tightly around her so that she can't move. He cradles her firmly in his arms while she weeps with anger and with frustration. He rocks her as she quiets down)*
FLOYD: I asked you a question.
STEPHEN: I think I better gather up my things and try to make it to a hotel.
FLOYD: You gather up nothing. Answer my question.
STEPHEN: *(After a beat)* No.
FLOYD: No what?
STEPHEN: We did nothing improper in your absence.
FLOYD: No hanky panky?
STEPHEN: That's correct.
FLOYD: Well, all I can say is you're pretty goddamn slow on the uptake. *(He releases her)*
Get me a refill, will you, honey?
(She moves quickly away from the men, repairs her make-up and prepares a drink for FLOYD)
(There is a pause)
DOLORES: Daddy thinks he's a comedian.
FLOYD: It's no joke. You spend all your time cooped up in here and don't get to meet many people. That's not so good for a girl your age. Is it, Steve?
STEPHEN: *(Agreeing with him)* I think it would be better if she met more people.
FLOYD: Right. That's what Dolores thinks, too. And I want her to have what she wants. Lately now, she's been talking to me a lot about romance. Do you know what I'm talking about? I'm trying not to be crude about this.
STEPHEN: *(After a beat)* Yes. I think I do.

FLOYD: Good.

DOLORES: Why don't we talk about something else?

(Beat)

Could I have some of that fish now?

STEPHEN: Good idea.

(To FLOYD)

How about you, sir? Can I fix you a little plate of herring?

FLOYD: Why don't you just call me Floyd.

(He looks carefully at STEPHEN)

Sure. I'll try some of your fancy food.

(He joins STEPHEN at the counter where he is setting out the contents of his cooler and basket: tinned anchovies, pickled herring, lettuce, tomato, vichyssoise, cantaloupe, tinned camembert, condiments, part of a loaf of dark rye bread)

You got any chocolate cake in there?

STEPHEN: No. Sorry.

FLOYD: Too bad. It's hard to have a birthday without a cake.

(To DOLORES)

Put out a couple of candles, why don't you, honey?

(She puts out a tattered tablecloth, some candles and some plates. She adjusts the lighting)

What's that stuff?

STEPHEN: Mustard.

FLOYD: Sure looks like shit to me.

(He turns to DOLORES)

Sorry.

(He holds up the open wine bottle and speaks to STEPHEN)

Is this what you're drinking?

STEPHEN: Yes.

FLOYD: Let me top you up.

(He overfills both glasses)

I want to propose a toast to my daughter on her 16th birthday, which is coming up Monday, but which we are celebrating tonight.

(STEPHEN and DOLORES exchange looks. He raises his whiskey glass to her)

To my birthday girl.

(STEPHEN and FLOYD drink a toast to her)

STEPHEN: To sweet 16.

FLOYD: You're goddamn right!

(STEPHEN hands DOLORES and FLOYD each a plate of food)

STEPHEN: I've left everything out. If you want more of anything, just help yourself.

(Silence)

(They eat)

DOLORES: This is good, Stephen.

FLOYD: Yeah. It's all right. Hey, you got any frog's legs in that cooler?

STEPHEN: No. I'm sorry.

FLOYD: Now, that's a real surprise to me. I'd have thought that cooler of yours would be chuck full of frog's legs. But maybe this is frog food he's feeding us. Is that right, Steve? Is this the same stuff you feed your frog hockey team? Is this the stuff that makes them skate so fast?

STEPHEN: Are you talking about the Montreal Canadiens?

FLOYD: No. I'm talking about the fucking frogs - the fucking frog hockey team. I was wondering if this was the stuff they eat. Hell, we don't stand on ceremony out here. Everybody just calls them the fucking frogs.

DOLORES: Do you want some more whiskey, Daddy?

FLOYD: Now you got no cause to get touchy with me, Steve. As far as I can see, I've been pretty goddamn hospitable to you. Especially when you consider I got very little stomach for you greedy Eastern bastards.

STEPHEN: Look, I'm not a banker.

FLOYD: You're not a what?

STEPHEN: I said I'm not a banker.

DOLORES: Stephen's a travelling salesman, Daddy. He sells diamonds and perfume.

FLOYD: *(To STEPHEN)* Sounds like a real manly occupation.
(Pause)
I'm not trying to put you down or anything.

STEPHEN: You'd be surprised, actually. It's more manly than you might think. Do you hunt?

FLOYD: Once in a while.

STEPHEN: That's manly, isn't it?

FLOYD: As long as you don't come home empty-handed, it is. Or smelling of perfume.

STEPHEN: I like a good hunt myself.

FLOYD: Rabbit?

STEPHEN: Sure, I've enjoyed going out after rabbit. In Europe, I've gone out quite often. We have a small factory at Baden-Baden and there are wild hare in the surrounding hills. It's mostly atmospheric, I suppose. Such a hunt. The right gun. A companionable dog. I prefer early morning while the air is still quiet.

FLOYD: Do you use a ferret?*(Beat)*

STEPHEN: *(Nonplussed)* I haven't, no. I think a ferret would spoil it for me. Unless, of course, sustenance were the issue.
(There is a long pause)
(No one is sure what to say next)

FLOYD: (Finally) Well, I'll leave you to it.
(He stands and downs the remainder of his beer. STEPHEN also stands as a courtesy)
I've got some things to catch up on in the shop.
(He exits)

COLD COMFORT

Jim Garrard

Place: as above
Time: as above
Characters: Dolores, Stephen

This two-character scene immediately follows Floyd's exit, above.

STEPHEN: *(After an interval)* Your dad doesn't like me very much, does he?

DOLORES: Oh, he's just jealous.

STEPHEN: How do you mean?

DOLORES: Well, he knows I like you quite a bit. He sees me having fun.

STEPHEN: Fun.

DOLORES: Yes.

STEPHEN: Do you think he's gone out there so that we can be alone?

DOLORES: I guess so. Partly. I mean, he's always going out to the shop to work on something.

STEPHEN: At 11 o'clock at night?

DOLORES: Sure. He usually has a nap after supper. But he works all the time. Except when he's watching TV or having his dinner.

STEPHEN: Was he serious what he said earlier?

DOLORES: What do you mean?

STEPHEN: What he said when he came back? After your bath?

DOLORES: About us?

STEPHEN: Yes.

DOLORES: Serious?

(She giggles)

You mean, does he really want you to get up on me?

STEPHEN: Yes.

DOLORES: It's hard living with a father who embarrasses you all the time.

(Pause)

He's been teasing me a lot lately that he was going to bring somebody home. That's because I complain all the time about never seeing anybody. He thinks I just mean boys. So he teases me about having only one thing on my mind.

STEPHEN: Do you?

DOLORES: Now you're embarrassing me.

STEPHEN: Don't be embarrassed. I just want to know what's expected of me.

DOLORES: I don't expect anything of you. Are you mad at me?

STEPHEN: No. What does your father expect of me?

DOLORES: I don't know.

STEPHEN: Do you have a boyfriend?

DOLORES: No. How could I? You're the first person I've talked to for more than five minutes for as long as I can remember.

STEPHEN: Haven't there been any other strangers that your father brought home?

DOLORES: No, there haven't. Why are you being mean to me all of a sudden?

STEPHEN: I'm not being mean. I just want to know what's going on. If I'm being set up for something, or not.

DOLORES: I don't know what you mean.

STEPHEN: Your father brings me here - you say you haven't talked to anybody for years - which is, therefore, an unusual, if not a unique piece of behavior on his part. He could have taken me into town to that hall which is what he did with the others. But he didn't. He brought me here to you, where he never brings anybody. He has, furthermore, implied that I should feel free to have sexual relations with his underage daughter and he doesn't even appear to like me. I think you better tell me what's going on here.

DOLORES: Nothing's going on. You don't have to do anything you don't want to.

STEPHEN: That's not my point. The point I'm trying to make is what do you and your father want me to do?

DOLORES: I just want you to have a good time. And I want you to like me.

STEPHEN: Look, suppose I ask you a direct question. Okay?

DOLORES: Okay.

STEPHEN: Will you give me a direct answer?

DOLORES: I'll try. What's the question?

STEPHEN: *(Choosing his words carefully)* Do you want me to fuck you?

DOLORES: *(After a pause)* That's pretty direct.

STEPHEN: That's not an answer.

DOLORES: Well, to tell you the truth, I'd like to find out what it's like. But I don't know if it would be possible.

STEPHEN: What do you mean?

DOLORES: I don't think I'd be able to do it.

STEPHEN: Why not?

DOLORES: I think I'm a little bit buggered up inside.

STEPHEN: Oh.

(Silence)

Buggered up in what way?

DOLORES: I think some of my parts are missing.

STEPHEN: What makes you think that?

DOLORES: When I was about eight, my Dad cut me open and took some stuff out.

STEPHEN: You're kidding me.

DOLORES: No. No, I'm not. Honest. You can look at the scar if you like. *(She draws back her dressing gown and lowers the waist of her pajamas to reveal an abdominal scar. He examines the scar closely, touches it and shakes his head)* I remember when he did it. He was in a terrible temper for days. He was mad at my mother about something. He gave me some chloroform, I think. When I woke up, I had bandages on my stomach and he wasn't mad any more. He was just kind. He was very kind to me.

STEPHEN: *(Finishing his examination of the scar)* God! What a horrible thing to do. Didn't they do anything to him?

DOLORES: Who?

STEPHEN: The authorities.

DOLORES: They don't know anything about it.

STEPHEN: But you must have seen a doctor. Surely.

DOLORES: There were no doctors. He just tied me down to the workbench and did it. I guess I was lucky I didn't die from all the bleeding.

STEPHEN: Or from the infection! God! God Almighty! Why did he do it?

DOLORES: I guess my mother was a pretty terrible person.

(Pause)

You know what she did once?

STEPHEN: What?

DOLORES: She put a piranha fish in Daddy's bathwater. I don't know for sure if it's true, but I heard him tell people that. He said he should have made her swallow it while it was still alive. Of course, that was a long time ago. He never talks about her any more.

STEPHEN: Is your mother dead?

DOLORES: She's not around, is she?

(He walks around the room, lost in thought)

(She looks at him appreciatively from time to time)

(They are silent)

STEPHEN: *(Finally)* I think you'd better come with me when I leave here in the morning.

DOLORES: Daddy wouldn't allow it.

STEPHEN: I don't see why we should give him any choice. Your dad doesn't seem to me to have looked after you very well so far. It's bad enough he keeps you a prisoner here.
(From across the room, with a wave of the hand, he indicates her abdomen)
But this! He ought to be in jail himself.

DOLORES: I'm not exactly a prisoner, you know. When I was younger, Daddy used to put a chain on my leg when he was away, but now he knows he doesn't have to. He never did. I wouldn't run away from him.

STEPHEN: How can you stay with a man who kept you chained up like a dog? What? Does he think he's a surgeon? Your father's crazy. He cuts open little girls' stomachs.

DOLORES: He had his reasons. He wouldn't hurt me now. I know he wouldn't.
(Pause)

STEPHEN: Are you going to stay here forever?

DOLORES: No. I hope not.

STEPHEN: When are you planning to leave?

DOLORES: I don't know yet.

STEPHEN: Come with me now. Tomorrow morning.

DOLORES: I can't.
(Pause)

STEPHEN: Why not?

DOLORES: I can't leave Daddy. I don't want him to be disappointed.

STEPHEN: Jesus Christ!

DOLORES: Anyway, where would you take me?

STEPHEN: Anywhere you like.

DOLORES: Anywhere?

STEPHEN: Anywhere.
(Beat)
(She sighs)

DOLORES: God!
(Pause)
Would I go with you to Montreal?

STEPHEN: If you like.

DOLORES: Would I go with you on trips? When you're doing your business?

STEPHEN: Whatever you like.

DOLORES: Even to New York City?

STEPHEN: Yes.

DOLORES: Why?

STEPHEN: Why what?

DOLORES: Why do you want to take me with you?

STEPHEN: I don't think you should stay here.

DOLORES: Is that the only reason?

STEPHEN: No, it isn't.
(Beat)
(They look directly at each other)
Not the only reason.
(Pause)
DOLORES: Will you take me everywhere with you?
STEPHEN: Yes.
DOLORES: Everywhere?
STEPHEN: Yes.
DOLORES: *(After a beat)* All right.
STEPHEN: You'll come?
DOLORES: Yes.
(Silence)
(She sheds a quantity of silent tears)
(He looks out at the weather)
STEPHEN: We'll go in the morning before it gets light. Is your father a sound sleeper?
DOLORES: Pretty sound. He snores real loud when he's had a few. Which is practically every night.
STEPHEN: Maybe you'd better gather up what you want to take with you. You can hide it in my suitcase. All right?
DOLORES: Sure. I don't have a lot of stuff.
STEPHEN: If they don't get the plough through, we may need to take the truck. Can you get the keys?
DOLORES: What about your car? You can't leave it.
STEPHEN: Yes we can. Can you get his keys?
DOLORES: He leaves them in the truck.
(She is packing. She goes in and out of the closet)
STEPHEN: In the ignition?
DOLORES: Yes.
(She speaks from inside the closet. She holds the clothesline and her underwear)
Damn!
STEPHEN: What's the matter?
DOLORES: This stuff is still wet.
STEPHEN: We can buy new things in the city. Check that they're still there if you get the chance, okay?
(She stares blankly at him)
The keys. Check that they're still in the ignition, okay?
DOLORES: Okay.
(He touches her gently and looks into her eyes)
STEPHEN: You're going to be glad, you know.
DOLORES: I hope so.
STEPHEN: Yes, you will.
(The blue light of an acetylene torch comes in through the glass in the shop

door. For the next few minutes, it reflects off the walls and ceiling near the door)

DOLORES: *(breaking the moment with STEPHEN)* I'd better hurry.

(She puts her wet laundry in a plastic bag and stuffs it into the suitcase)

STEPHEN: *(Packing up the cooler and the basket)* I think we can slip this stuff back in the car. Do you? Can you do it?

DOLORES: Sure. In a minute.

(She brings a few items of clothing from her closet-bedroom and toilet utensils from the bathroom. She crams these into the suitcase. They are both intensely aware of Floyd's presence on the other side of the door and the possibility of sudden discovery)

It's hard to know what to take and what to leave behind.

(She finds herself standing near STEPHEN. She is perplexed. She kisses him suddenly on the cheek, impulsively. She laughs)

It's funny, isn't it?

STEPHEN: Yes, it is.

DOLORES: I'd better take this.

(She takes the cooler and basket into service bays, leaving the door open)

THE CRACK-WALKER

Judith Thompson

Place: Sandy and Joe's apartment, Kingston
Time: evening
Characters: Theresa, Sandy

After an incident at the care home in which she was staying (she was caught in her room with a naked man), the marginally retarded Theresa runs away and shows up at Sandy and Joe's apartment. Joe is a thug who makes his living by stealing things—motorcycles, for example— and selling them "hot." Sandy is his girlfriend, upset at Joe's many infidelities and worried that she is losing her looks.

As this scene opens, Sandy is scrubbing the floor. Theresa enters, carrying a plastic bag.

SANDY: What are you doin here?
THERESA: I come callin on ya!
(In the following sequence, SANDY's anger builds. At first, however, it contains an element of teasing)
SANDY: I don't want no houndogs callin on me. *(Continues scrubbing)*
THERESA: I not a houndog!
SANDY: Yes, y'are.
THERESA: No I not.
SANDY: Whoredog houndog that's what you are.
THERESA: *(Laughs, delighted)* Sanny!
SANDY: *(Pointing backwards)* And get your whorepaws offa my sofa.
THERESA: *(Jumps, removes hand, gasps)* Sanny, like I don't mean to bug ya or nothin *(Eating doughnut from bag)* but like I don't get off on livin where I'm living no more so I come back here sleepin on the couch, okay?

SANDY: I not keeping no cowpies here.

THERESA: I not a cowpie!

SANDY: *(Faces her)* Would you get out of my house?

THERESA: Why, what I done?

SANDY: ... Ya smell like cookin fat - turns my gut.

THERESA: That only cause I eatin chip from the chipwagon!

SANDY: I don't care what it's cause of, get your whoreface out of here.

THERESA: Why, why you bein ugly for?

SANDY: You tell me and then we'll both know.

THERESA: What.

SANDY: Don't think nobody seen ya neither cause Bonnie Cain seen
ya right through the picture window!
(THERESA claps a hand to her mouth as in "uh-oh")
On my couch that I paid for with my money.

THERESA: Wha -

SANDY: With MY HUSBAND!

THERESA: No way, Sanny.

SANDY: *(Unable to contain her anger any longer)* You touch my fuckin
husband again and I break every bone in your body!

THERESA: Bonnie Cain lyin she lyin to ya she think I took 20 buck off
her she trying to get me back.

SANDY: *(Starts speaking after "she lyin to ya")* That's bullshit Therese
cause Bonnie Cain don't lie and you know she don't.

THERESA: You don't trus me.

SANDY: Fuckin right.

THERESA: I never done it.

SANDY: Pretty bad combination, Trese, a retarded whore.

THERESA: That's a load of bullshit Sanny, I NOT RETARDED.

SANDY: Just get out of my house and don't come back. *(Pushes her)*

THERESA: NO I NEVER I never done it! *(In angry indignation she pushes
back)*

SANDY: Trese Joe told me, he told me what the two of youse done!

THERESA: Oh.

SANDY: Lyin whore, look at ya ya make me sick. Wearin that ugly dress
thinkin it's sexy cause it shows off your fat tits and those shoes are
fuckin stupid ya can't even walk in them.

THERESA: I know.
(SANDY stares at THERESA. THERESA does not move)

SANDY: *(With an air of resignation, tiredness)* Just get out, okay?

THERESA: I never wanted it, Sanny, I never wanted it he come in he
made me.

SANDY: Bull Trese.

THERESA: He did I sleepin I sleepin there havin dreams I seen this
puppy and he come in and tie me up and push it in me down my hole.

SANDY: What?

THERESA: He tie me all up with strings and that and he singin Ol Madonel Farm and he say he gonna kill me if I don't shut up so I be quiet and he done it he screw me.

SANDY: Are you shittin me?

THERESA: And - and - and he singing and he take his jean down and it all hard and smellin like pee pee and he go and he put it in my mouth.

SANDY: He could do 20 for that.

THERESA: Don't send him up the river Sanny he didn't mean nothin.

SANDY: Horny bastard he's not gettin into me again.

THERESA: Me neither Sanny he tries anything I just run up to Tim Horton's get a fancy doughnut.

SANDY: Oh he won't be cheatin on me again.

THERESA: How come Sanny, you tell him off?

SANDY: Fuckin right I did. After Bonnie tole me, I start givin him shit, eh, and he takes the hand to me callin me a hag and sayin how he liked pokin you better'n that and look. *(Reveals bruise)*

THERESA: Bassard.

SANDY: He's done it before, but he won't do it again.

THERESA: Why, Sanny, you call the cops on him?

SANDY: RIGHT.

THERESA: Did ya -

SANDY: Ya know my high heels? The shiny black ones I got up in Toronto?

THERESA: Yeah, they're sharp.

SANDY: *(Obviously enjoys telling the story)* And he knows it, too. After he beat up on me he takes off drinkin, comes back about three just shitfaced, eh, and passes out cold? Well I'm there lookin at him snorin like a pig and I says to myself "I'm gonna get this bastard." I'm thinkin of how when I seen my heels sittin over in the corner and then I know what I'm gonna do. So I take one of the heels and go over real quiet to where he lyin, and ya know what I do? I take the heel and I rip the holy shit out of his back with it.

THERESA: JEEZ DID HE WAKE UP?

SANDY: Fuckin right he did. You shoulda seen him, first I guess he thought he was dreamin, eh, so he just lies there makin these ugly noises burpin and that? And then he opens his eyes, and puts his hands up like a baby eh, and THEN I SEEN him SEE the heel. Well I take off right out the back door and he's comin after me fit to kill his eyes is all red he's hissin I am scared shitless; well he gets ahold of me and I says to myself "Sandy this is it. This is how you're gonna die. You got the bastard back and now you're gonna die for it." Well he is just about to send me to the fuckin angels when he stops; just like that and turns around and goes on to bed.

THERESA: How come he done that, Sanny?

SANDY: I didn't know at first either, then I figured it out. Cuttin him with the heel was the smartest thing I done. Ya see, he wasn't gonna kill me cause he don't want to do time, eh, and he knew if he just beat up on me he'd never get no more sleep cause I'd do it again. He knows it. He don't dare take a hand to me again, no way. Either he takes off, or he stays and he treats me nice.

THERESA: Did you talk to him later?

SANDY: I ain't seen him for three days. But we ate together before he took off, I fixed him up some tuna casserole and we ate it; we didn't say nothin, though. It don't matter, we sometimes go a whole week without talkin, don't mean we're pissed off at each other.

THERESA: Al and I talkin all the time when we go out.

SANDY: We did too when we first started goin together. After a while ya don't have to talk cause you always know what they're gonna say anyways. Makes ya sick sometimes. What are you bawlin for?

THERESA: I'm sorry Joe done that to me, Sanny.

SANDY: He's like that, he's a prick.

THERESA: S'okay if I come livin here then?

SANDY: ... Sure, I don't care.

THERESA: Thank you Sanny.

SANDY: I like the company.

THERESA: Don't say nothin to Al, eh?

SANDY: What if I tell him what Bonnie Cain tole me about you blowin off queers down the Lido?

THERESA: Oh no, Sanny, don't say bout that.

SANDY: I guess old fags in Kingston are pretty hard up.

THERESA: You want a doughnut, Sanny?

SANDY: No. What kind ya got.

THERESA: Apple fritters.

SANDY: Jeez, Therese, ya ever see how they make them things?

THERESA: No, I never worked up there.

SANDY: It'd make ya sick.

THERESA: I love em.

SANDY: I know ya do, you're a pig.

THERESA: Fuck off ... Only kiddin.

SANDY: You watch your mouth.

THERESA: You love Joe still?

SANDY: I don't know. I used to feel like we was in the fuckin movies. Member that show Funny Girl where Barbra Streisand and Omar Sharif are goin together?

THERESA: She hardly sing pretty.

SANDY: Well remember that part where they start singin right on the boat, singin to each other?

THERESA: Yeah.

SANDY: We done that once. We'd been up at the Manor, eh, Chesty

Morgan was up there so we'd just been havin a hoot, eh, and Joe wants to go over to the General Wolfe to see the Major, so we get on the Wolfe Island ferry and we're laughin and carryin on and that and then we start singin, right on the bow of the Wolfe Island ferry.

THERESA: Jeez.

SANDY: We didn't care when we were doin it though, we didn't give a shit what anyone was thinkin, fuck 'em we were havin fun.

THERESA: I love singin.

SANDY: Joe really done that to you?

THERESA: What?

SANDY: RAPED ya.

THERESA: Don't like talkin about it Sanny.

SANDY: TRESE.

THERESA: He done it when I never wanted it it's true.

SANDY: It is, eh?

THERESA: S'true, Sanny. Don't tell Joe, eh?

SANDY: I mighta known it.

THERESA: Still okay if I sleepin here though?

SANDY: You're gonna have to do the housework while I'm workin for Nikos.

THERESA: How come you workin down there I thought you didn't like Nikos?

SANDY: I get off on cornbeef on rye, arswipe, what d'ya think I need the fuckin money.

THERESA: Ain't Joe drivin for Amey's no more?

SANDY: No.

THERESA: What's he doin?

SANDY: Fuckin the dog, I don't know.

THERESA: Bassard.

SANDY: I know. Gimme a bite of that.

THERESA: I not really retarded am I Sanny?

SANDY: Just a little slow.

THERESA: Not like that guy walkin downstreet lookin at the sidewalk?

SANDY: Jeez he give me the creeps.

THERESA: He hardly got the long beard, eh?

SANDY: I know.

THERESA: Not like him, eh Sanny?

SANDY: No. No, I tole ya Therese, you're just a little slow.

THE CRACK-WALKER

Judith Thompson

Place: a restaurant, Kingston
Time: unspecified
Characters: Theresa, Al

Shortly after Al finds out that his girlfriend Theresa and his best buddy
   Joe have slept together, he forgives them. Al is the underconfident,
   forgiving type. He lives his life vicariously through Joe. Any unpleas-
   antness that Joe has caused him Al simply tries to forget.

Theresa and Al are sitting in a restaurant.

THERESA: Where d'ya think Joe took off to?
ALAN: I don't know probably drinkin, maybe the Shamrock.
THERESA: You think they're splitting up?
ALAN: I hope not.
THERESA: Me too. I love Sandy, she my best girlfriend.
ALAN: I - Joe - he and me are good buddies too. They go good together
   anyways.
THERESA: Could I have a doughnut?
ALAN: What kind, chocolate? I know you like chocolate.
THERESA: I love it.
ALAN: Sandy's nuts, you're not fat.
THERESA: Don't say nothin about it.
ALAN: You're not.
THERESA: I don't like talkin about it.
ALAN: Here. Two chocolate doughnuts.
THERESA: Thank you Alan.
ALAN: Jesus you're a good lookin girl. You're the prettiest lookin girl
   I seen.

THERESA: Don't talk like that.

ALAN: I love screwin with ya. Do you like it with me?

THERESA: I don't know - don't ask me that stuff dummy-face.

ALAN: I like eatin ya out ya know.

THERESA: Shut your mouth people are lookin don't talk like that stupid-face.

ALAN: Nobody's lookin. Jeez you're pretty. Just like a little angel. Huh. Like a - I know. I know. I'm gonna call you my little angel from now on. People gonna see ya and they're gonna go "There's Trese, she's Al's angel."

THERESA: Who gonna say them things?

ALAN: Anybody.

THERESA: They are?

ALAN: Yup.

THERESA: You're a dummy-face.

ALAN: So beautiful.

THERESA: Stop it Al you make me embarrass.

ALAN: You're - I was always hopin for someone like you - always happy always laughin and that.

THERESA: I cryin sometimes ya know.

ALAN: Yeah but ya cry the same way ya laugh. There's somethin - I don't know - as soon as I seen ya I knew I wanted ya. I wanted to marry ya when I seen ya.

THERESA: When, when did you say that?

ALAN: I never said nothin, I just thought it, all the time.

THERESA: We only been goin together for a little while, you know.

ALAN: Let's get married.

THERESA: Al stop lookin at me like that you embarrassin me.

ALAN: Sorry. Did you hear me?

THERESA: Yeah. Okay.

ALAN: When.

THERESA: Tuesday. I ask my sosha worker to come.

ALAN: No. Just Joe and me and you and Sandy. Just the four of us. I want Joe to be my best man.

THERESA: Sandy could be the flower girl. Uh. Oh.

ALAN: What?

THERESA: Hope you don't want no babies.

ALAN: Why. I do! I do want babies! I get on with babies good!

THERESA: Not sposda have none.

ALAN: How come? Who told you that?

THERESA: The sosha worker, she say I gotta get my tubes tied.

ALAN: What's that?

THERESA: Operation up the hospital. They tie it up down there so ya won't go havin babies.

ALAN: They can't do that to you no way!

THERESA: I know they can't but they're doin it.

ALAN: They don't have no RIGHT.

THERESA: Yah they do Al I slow.

ALAN: Slow? I don't think you're slow who told you that?

THERESA: I ain't a good mum Al I can't help it.

ALAN: Who said you ain't a good mum.

THERESA: All of them jus cause when I took off on Dawn.

ALAN: Who's Dawn?

THERESA: The baby, the other baby.

ALAN: You never had a baby before did ya? Did ya?

THERESA: Las -

ALAN: You didn't have no other man's baby did ya? With another guy?
(Pause)

THERESA: No, it's Bernice's.

ALAN: Who's Bernice.

THERESA: My cousin my mum's sister.

ALAN: Well how come you were looking after her baby?

THERESA: Cause she was sick up in hospital. Jeez Al.

ALAN: Well - what happened what'dja do wrong?

THERESA: Nothin it wasn't my fault just one Friday night I was sniffin, eh, so I took off down to the plaza and I leave the baby up the room, eh, I thought I was comin right back, and I met this guy and he buyin me drinks and that then I never knew what happened and I woke up and I asked somebody where I was and I was in Ottawa!

ALAN: He took you all the way up to Ottawa? That bastard.

THERESA: I never seen him again I thumbed back to Kingston. *(Crying)* I come back to the house and baby's gone she ain't there so I bawlin I goin everywhere yellin after her and never found nothin then I see Bonnie Cain and she told me they took her up the Children's Aid she dead. So I go on up the Aid and they say she ain't dead she live but they not givin her back cause I unfit.

ALAN: Jeez.

THERESA: I ain't no more Al I don't sniff or nothin.

ALAN: Them bastards.

THERESA: Honest.

ALAN: I know. I know ya don't and we're gonna have a baby and nobody ain't gonna stop us. We're gonna have our own little baby between you and me and nobody can't say nothin bout it. You're not goin to no hospital, understand?

THERESA: But Al she say she gonna cut off my pension check if I don't get my tubes tied.

ALAN: Fuck the pension check you're not goin to no hospital.

THERESA: Okay Al.

ALAN: Come here. You're not goin to no hospital.

THERESA: You won't let em do nothing to me, will ya Al?

ALAN: Nope. You're my angel and they ain't gonna touch you ... Hey! I know what ya look like now!

THERESA: What, an angel?

ALAN: That - that madonna lady you know them pictures they got up in classrooms when you're a kid? Them pictures of the madonna?

THERESA: The Virgin Mary?

ALAN: Yeah. Her.

THERESA: I love her I askin her for stuff.

ALAN: Yuh look just like her. Just like the madonna. Cept the madonna picture got a baby in it.

THERESA: It do?

ALAN: She's holdin it right in her arms. You too, maybe, eh? Eh? Hey! Let's go up to the Good Thief.

THERESA: Al I don't know you goin to church! You goin every Sunday?

ALAN: No I never went since I was five I just want to go now. We'll go and we'll - we'll like have a party lightin candles and that a party for gettin married!

THERESA: I love lightin candles.

ALAN: Maybe the Father's gonna be there. They're always happy when someone's gettin married we could tell him!

THERESA: Al I gettin sleepy.

ALAN: Well after we party I'm gonna put ya right down to sleep over at Joe's. I won't try nothin or nothin.

THERESA: What if Sandy be piss off.

ALAN: No Trese, they said we could stay there together. The two of us. And we're gonna.

THERESA: Okay ... really I lookin like that madonna?

ALAN: Just like her. Just like her.

(He is rocking her in his arms. Lights fade)

CRUEL TEARS

Ken Mitchell and Humphrey & the Dumptrucks

Place: Earl's office, Saskatoon
Time: May or June, 1974
Characters: Jack Deal, 30; Earl Jensen, 45, owner of Motormack Express

This scene echoes Shakespeare's *Othello*, Act I, scene i. Johnny Roychuck, a 28 year-old truck driver and a Ukrainian-Canadian, happens to be in love with the boss's daughter. Jack Deal is the Iago figure; supposedly a friend of Johnny's, he is jealous of his buddy's success with women and work. Unlike Iago, whose allegations are made anonymously to Brabantio, Jack approaches the trucking company boss Earl Jensen in a seemingly forthright manner. But his intimations that Johnny has seduced Earl's daughter are almost as lewd and provocative as Iago's famous line: "an old black ram/ Is tupping your white yew." Whereas Brabantio is slow to forgive, Earl will later relent rather easily and bless the marriage of his daughter Kathy and Johnny Roychuck.

The lights go up on EARL Jensen working inside at his desk. JACK knocks at his "door"
EARL: Yeah - who is it?
JACK: *(Stepping inside)* Yuh free for a minnit, Mr. Jensen?
EARL: What's on your mind, Deal?
JACK: It's about the contract, Mr. Jensen.
EARL: Contract talks are in September. You better see me then.
JACK: Well, the boys are havin' it pretty tough with all this inflation. Cost a livin's goin' up alla time!
EARL: Cost? Don't tell ME about cost!
   (He shows JACK the clipboard he has been working on)
   There's the fuel bill for this outfit last month.
   (JACK looks. He whistles sympathetically)
   That's right - you guys never see it from my viewpoint.
JACK: How about OUR viewpoint? We gotta LIVE. It isn't just a matter

of balancin' books, you know. We got kids to feed -

EARL: Every driver in the company signed that contract - !

JACK: Yeah, we signed, Mr. Jensen, but if it means we hafta work to rule just to get our fair share - well -

EARL: That sounds like UNION talk to me, Deal.

JACK: No unions here, Mr. Jensen.

EARL: That's right. Your job was to keep the Teamsters OUT.

JACK: Yeah - okay.
(He shrugs and grins)
Can't blame a guy for tryin'. We gotta keep the boys happy, don't we?

EARL: *(Getting out a bottle of whiskey)* That's right, Deal. Humor the boys. Have a slug?

JACK: Say no more!
(EARL pours a drink for JACK. A pause. JACK toasts him)
Well - management wins again!
(JACK laughs and drinks. EARL turns back to his work waiting for JACK to leave. JACK sets his glass down)

EARL: What now?

JACK: Well. I uh - don't know how to start - I'm not very good at talking about this kinda thing - I guess it's best to just come right to the point, not beat around the bush -

EARL: What's the problem now?

JACK: Oh, there's no problem - with the company. It's uh sorta - personal - matter.

EARL: *(Indignant)* Personal?

JACK: Yuh see, there's this - talk goin' around the depot, and it's - well, kinda gross.

EARL: *(Standing)* Get to the point!

JACK: Well - this story - I won't mention any names - has it there's a sweet little girl from the suburbs involved in some pretty funny business on the other side of town -

EARL: *(Impatient)* So?

JACK: It's a real sideshow. You know - animal act - like the kinda stuff you were tellin' us YOU saw down in Vegas.
(He grins)
Remember?

EARL: Yeah?

JACK: Yeah! Over on the other side a the river! I know you don't get into that part of town much, Mr. Jensen - lotta DPs, yuh know. Indians. But there's this big dumb bohunk over there who's got a PERFECT set-up - yuh know, bachelor pad, lotsa booze, the whole bit -

EARL: AND?

JACK: And this sweet little chick from the suburbs gets the blocks put to her by the bohunk - every night, when her old man thinks she's at her pottery class!

EARL: *(Stunned)* What?

JACK: So this story goes.

(A pause)

EARL: KATHARINE?

JACK: *(Hastily)* No, Earl - NO. It's just GOSSIP, like I said. I only mentioned it because I thought maybe you should - put a stop to it -

EARL: It's a lie!

JACK: Sure - I know it's a lie. I wouldn't even a repeated it - but you gotta face facts. It's the kinda thing could ruin Kathy's reputation fer good.

EARL: *(Getting hold of himself)* Who - told you this?

JACK: Let's see, I guess it musta bin Ricky. What was it the hippie said? "Now she's used goods, man."

(EARL reacts to this)

Course, nobody ever believes a thing he says anyway. Just a loud-mouth - you know the kind. Always lookin' fer the worst in people.

EARL: I'll put a stop to this nonsense right away.

(A pause)

I appreciate it, Jack.

JACK: Appreciate?

EARL: Your - honesty. And, uh - one more thing. Who's the - culprit?

(A long pause)

JACK: Now, that's askin' a bit much, Earl. Don't forget I gotta WORK with these guys.

EARL: ONE OF MY DRIVERS?

JACK: Well - I don't wanta get anybody in trouble. Maybe there's nuthin' to this. You see, in my position -

EARL: What's it worth to you?

JACK: I didden come here fer money, EARL.

EARL: *(Angrily)* Well, what did you come for?

(A pause. JACK shrugs)

JACK: *(Smiling)* The cost-a-livin' hike? Remember?

EARL: *(Pausing)* Okay. Ten percent, across the board!

(A pause)

And your usual commission.

JACK: I can't rat on a driver, Earl!

EARL: Who is it?

(A pause. JACK looks pained)

JACK: No, I just can't do it. Not to a buddy.

EARL: ROYCHUK? I'll - !

JACK: Hey, take it EASY, Earl!

EARL: I - I'll look after this now.

(In control)

I can destroy this - rotten lie.

(A pause. EARL pours two drinks)

Of course, none of this discussion will leave the office.

JACK: Right you are, Earl.*(JACK salutes and drinks his whiskey)* I'll, uh, move along then.

EARL: *(Distantly)* Okay.

JACK: *(Going out)* And I'll bring that contract down next week! For your John Henry.

CUBISTIQUE
Tom Cone

Time: early 1920s
Place: a salon in Paris
Characters: Francis, Annie

Cubistique is, in style and content, reminiscent of the prose of
Gertrude Stein. The significance attached to role-playing in Cone's
one-act is, perhaps, an extension of point of view in *The Autobiogra-
phy of Alice B. Toklas*, in which Stein assumes the persona of her real-
life secretary. Like Stein, Cone allows himself to be influenced by
other art forms besides literature. His methodology for the develop-
ment of character is borrowed from the Cubists. We see Francis and
Annie from a multitude of perspectives—through mirror images,
direct analysis and action, and outright mimicry. Setting his play in
a Parisian salon in the 1920s, Cone intimates that the relationship
of Francis and Annie may be based on the historical relationship of
Stein and Toklas. There are also intimations that, like their models,
Francis and Annie are lovers.

Francis is English, 35 years old, and hostess of her own salon. Annie is
an American who seems, at first, naive. As the playwright maintains,
however, Annie emanates an underlying sexuality "that is somehow
teasing, but real."

As this opening scene of the play begins, Francis and Annie are standing
in a freeze position, mirroring one another. Francis is teaching Annie
how to pronounce the word "mange" correctly. (A third character in
the scene is the piano player, who does not speak but who plays and
stops playing at Francis' command.)

FRANCIS: Good. Now again.
  (FRANCIS is trying to teach ANNIE the "a" in "Mange")
FRANCIS and ANNIE: *(Together, and exaggerated)* M-a-n-g-e ... m-a-n-
  g-e ...
  (This continues until ANNIE actually produces the right sound)
ANNIE: *(Smiling)* Merde!
  (FRANCIS moves to the other side of ANNIE)

FRANCIS: Good! Now, together ...

FRANCIS and ANNIE: *(Together)* Mange merde.

ANNIE: Francis, this is ridiculous!

FRANCIS: *(Exaggerated; uses two fingers to open ANNIE's mouth)* M-a-n-g-e.

FRANCIS and ANNIE: *(Together)* Mange.

FRANCIS: Aah, Annie, you will have it in no time.

ANNIE: What? Repeating "mange merde" all over the streets? Oh Francis, don't you think there are other expressions ...? *(Laughing to herself)* I'm sorry, but when you take your fingers and pry the syllables from my mouth, especially that phrase ...

FRANCIS: ... "a" ... "e" ...
(As in "mange" and "merde")

ANNIE: Yes, the sound is gorgeous and the texture of the syllables is lovely ... but the meaning? Now, Francis, don't you think it's a bit ludicrous, or should I say, vicarious?

FRANCIS: What?
(ANNIE is smiling, takes her own fingers and opens her mouth lowly to say "mange." FRANCIS is now preparing the coffee)

FRANCIS: Sucre?

ANNIE: Non, merci.

FRANCIS: ... "u" ... "o" ... "e" ...
(As in "sucre," "non" and "merci")

ANNIE: I spent half a day looking around for a salon gown. I must have been to 30 shops trying to figure out what would be appropriate. *(With a sense of discovery)* I thought of the city, then the length ... I thought of the time of day, then the color ... and finally I decided that I must think what you would be serving for lunch ... so I would compliment the dessert!

FRANCIS: Peche melba?

ANNIE: Yes.

FRANCIS: A divine soprano!

ANNIE: Then you like the gown?

FRANCIS: No, no ... why, yes my dear.

ANNIE: Every merchant in town kept asking me ... *(With a French accent)* "Madame, I do not know what a salon gown is. Please, can you tell me where it is you are going, and maybe I can help you, no?" I told them your name ...

FRANCIS: Yes?
(Pause)

ANNIE: And what I thought you would be serving ...

FRANCIS: No, no!

ANNIE: And ...

FRANCIS: Go on - what did they say?

ANNIE: When? Oh! Just that ...

(Begins to smile to herself)

FRANCIS: Go ahead ... Annie! What is it they said? *(Inhaling)* Forget it! I don't care. Those damn merchants, they're more interested in spreading a little second-hand gossip than spreading a gown over your body ... and all the talk about them being ...

ANNIE: *(With a French accent)* "Ma-dame Francis? Aahhh ... a special gown you will need."

FRANCIS: What do you mean ... "a special gown"? *(Composing herself)* The invitation clearly stated, "Luncheon at two o'clock," with a postscript offering you a small lesson in the phonetics of the French language ... Now what ...

ANNIE: "More than a salon gown."

FRANCIS: Could be so important ...?

ANNIE: "As you say, Ma-dame."

FRANCIS: What?!

ANNIE: "You will need more ..."
(She giggles)

FRANCIS: *(Staring at her)* I do not ...

ANNIE and FRANCIS: *(Together)* ... know ... what ...
(ANNIE is mimicking FRANCIS)

FRANCIS: Annie?

FRANCIS and ANNIE: *(Together)* ... you mean?
(ANNIE mimics FRANCIS again)

FRANCIS: What are you doing? Is this a behavior that becomes an invitation? I believe, my dear, there was a time when I taught you that mimicry can suggest more than light sarcasm. Upon first impression, one could say there was not so hidden bitterness, but upon further investigation ... a jealousy could be revealed. It is a two-part lesson ...

ANNIE: FRANCIS?

FRANCIS: That needs a careful and ...

ANNIE: IF I was to say yes ...

FRANCIS: One moment! A careful and respectful looking over. Now, what were you saying?

ANNIE: If I was to say yes ...

FRANCIS: What about?

ANNIE: That I am jealous of you. What would you say?

FRANCIS: That is a hypothetical question.

ANNIE: Yes?

FRANCIS: And one is unable to honestly answer such things.

ANNIE: Hypothetical questions?

FRANCIS: Yes! *(Short pause)* What are you talking about? *(Short pause)* I feel chilly. Come here ... *(Arms out)* Hold my hands.
(ANNIE does so. FRANCIS leans close)

FRANCIS: And we'll try to answer ... hypothetical ... questions ...

together. Yes? Annie?

(FRANCIS breaks away and turns)

FRANCIS: I would want to know why you are jealous of me. What it really is ... that you are jealous of.

(Slightly turned, waiting for answer, apprehensive)

FRANCIS: Annie?

ANNIE: *(Calmly)* Style.

FRANCIS: I, well ... that is not something to be ...

ANNIE: Your style, Francis ...

(A short pause. ANNIE stares. FRANCIS stares back, then seems to think of something. A smile appears on her face and she turns)

FRANCIS: If it's style that you're jealous of ... I don't quite understand, well ... perhaps I agree ...

ANNIE: How so?

FRANCIS: I think it began when you once said something about ... Oh yes! Let me see how I ... OH, FRANCIS! YOU ARE THE FIRST LADY TO VISIT AMERICA WEARING A PINKY RING!

ANNIE: Oh Francis! That ...

FRANCIS: THAT was a sign of ...

ANNIE: Jealousy?

FRANCIS: Yes. Now ...

ANNIE: But ...

FRANCIS: One moment. And do you remember when I was about to return to Europe and we discussed the importance of a sense of good timing?

ANNIE: And you felt three years in America would ... KEEP ME MORE THAN AHEAD OF JUST HEMLINES AND MONARCHS!

FRANCIS: *(Cutting in)* Two important indications in the seeding of a jealousy.

ANNIE: Hemlines and monarchs?

FRANCIS: Entrances and exits, my dear.

ANNIE: What?

FRANCIS: Knowing what to wear when you arrive ... *(Turning her pinky ring)* And how long to stay. *(Smiles)* Now we can begin to ...

ANNIE: One moment please! If you don't mind I'd like to explain what I meant.

FRANCIS: But I know perfectly well what you ...

ANNIE: Why do you always interrupt? And then change the direction where it suits you?

FRANCIS: Were we not discussing your jealousy ... of my style?

ANNIE: Of course.

FRANCIS: And don't you think I'm aware of ...

ANNIE: Francis? *(Smiling)* I've changed my mind.

FRANCIS: Well, you just can't do that!

ANNIE: I am not jealous of your style.

FRANCIS: You just told me ...

ANNIE: Hypothetical question.

FRANCIS: I do not believe you!

ANNIE: Well ... how can I convince you? It's very easy. *(Slow)* I simply am not jealous of you.

FRANCIS: *(Trying to gain composure, hands out)* Tell me ... what do you see?

ANNIE: *(Confused)* What?

FRANCIS: What do you see?

ANNIE: You.

FRANCIS: No, no ... look carefully. What do you really see?

ANNIE: *(Looking away)* Thirty-five years.

FRANCIS: *(Begins to smile)* Go on.

ANNIE: *(Coy)* What do YOU want?

FRANCIS: *(Begins to slowly model)* Go ... on ...

ANNIE: *(Staring)* I see a friend ...

FRANCIS: Yes?

ANNIE: Who ... *(Quickly)* ... needs to know what she looks like! I don't know. What am I supposed to say?

FRANCIS: Continue.

ANNIE: *(Begins to move around FRANCIS)* Five foot, six ... *(Smiling)* Legs like sticks ...
(Touches FRANCIS's hemline)

FRANCIS: Annie!

ANNIE: Dressed in an attire suitable ... *(Staring)* ... only for that person.

FRANCIS: And that person?

ANNIE: A vulnerable one.

FRANCIS: Care to explain?

ANNIE: Look! It's just a feeling. You asked me what I saw ... *(Notices FRANCIS staring, waiting)* All right! *(To herself)* Vulnerable ... it's not something to be offended by! It's just I see how vulnerable you really are. What's wrong with that?

FRANCIS: Nothing.

ANNIE: Francis. I don't mind seeing your vulnerability ...

FRANCIS: *(Resigning)* That's fine ... *(short pause)* Now. *(Looking ANNIE over)* May I observe?

ANNIE: Of course not! Those are your silly games and I do not want to be a guinea pig for any of them.

FRANCIS: Guinea pig?

ANNIE: American.

FRANCIS: *(Caricature of ANNIE)* Style.

ANNIE: *(Caricature of FRANCIS)* Mimicry, my dear ...
(They both laugh. Short pause)

FRANCIS: I've got an idea. Why don't we pretend each other's style and then see ourselves by looking at the other?

ANNIE: I don't quite ...

FRANCIS: I'll show you.

ANNIE: But Francis!

FRANCIS: Just a moment. Let me think.
(She moves away with her back turned, then slowly faces ANNIE once more, doing an imitation of ANNIE's movements as well as her voice)

FRANCIS: Oh, Francis! A wonderful thing happened today. Oh, I don't know how to tell you about it ... I'm sure I will if you let me ... *(Smiling)*

ANNIE: I'm not sure that I ...

FRANCIS: The streets were full of people, so many colors to look at, and they were all, somehow I felt ... all of them ...

ANNIE: Francis!

FRANCIS: *(Continuing)* ... looking at me! *(Drops the caricature, walks to ANNIE)* What do you think?

ANNIE: Are you being Francis now? Or ... are you being ...

FRANCIS and ANNIE: *(Together)* Me.

FRANCIS: I'm me, of course. Oh dear, don't look so disappointed. Next time I will practise and do a much better job.

ANNIE: At what?

FRANCIS: At playing you, of course. Now ... it's your turn. Let's see you give me a chance. Walk across the room ... then.

ANNIE: Francis! I can prepare without your ...

FRANCIS: I was just trying to help.

ANNIE: *(Walks across the room, over her shoulder)* Ready? *(Takes a step and quickly turns around, into her caricature of FRANCIS)* If there are two things that I so dislike ... they are impatience and ... passivity.

FRANCIS: What are you saying?

ANNIE: Impatience, I'm sure, derives from a hurried weaning that ...

FRANCIS: Annie!

ANNIE: ... comes from a lack of respect for the child.

FRANCIS: What?!

ANNIE: And passivity ...

FRANCIS: *(Walks right up to ANNIE)* Yes?

ANNIE: ... is born out of cynical mating. How did I do?

FRANCIS: I'm not sure. I ... *(Pause)* You see me like that? A woman spouting polarities?

ANNIE: Those that are aware of the polarity, ironically, are not in balance ... but carry the weight of contradiction.

FRANCIS: What a memory!

ANNIE: *(Moving away)* Why don't we try a dialogue? I think I'm beginning to enjoy your game. So, you still will be me and I you and we'll try acting each other as if we were having a conversation. *(Sits on the settee)*

ANNIE: Come here, Annie. Sit by me.

(FRANCIS does so, reluctantly)

ANNIE: Now, tell me abut your day. We've practised this question, remember? Go on ...

(Short pause)

FRANCIS: *(Struggling with caricature)* It was confusing ... I had to find a gown for the occasion ...

ANNIE: Yes, go on. Where did you go?

FRANCIS: Many shops. I had gone to many shops looking for a salon gown to wear this afternoon.

ANNIE: It looks as if you succeeded in finding one.

FRANCIS: Oh, just a modest gown, but the proprietor felt that since I was coming to Madame Francis' salon I must remember ... *(Quickly)* ... chic-chic-chic!

ANNIE: *(Noticing her own gown)* Yes, well, perhaps you would care for a glass of liqueur?

FRANCIS: Of course. That would be lovely.

ANNIE: *(Gets up, but can't find the cabinet)* How boring of me ... I can't seem to find the ...

FRANCIS: You haven't had visitors for a long time I presume.

ANNIE: Just a reflective period. Excuse me while I look for the ...

FRANCIS: Oh! Creme de cacao if you have some.

ANNIE: What?!

FRANCIS: Oh, it's become a favorite of mine in the afternoon now. So many of my friends suggested anisette before coming to Europe, but the Cacao reminds me so much of ...

ANNIE: Oh! Pardon me. I didn't realize the strong affinity to ...

FRANCIS: My childhood. Oh, I had a friend who introduced me to cacao. It was so many years ago ...

ANNIE: Yes. Well, do you recall her ...?

FRANCIS: I have forgotten her name. Now if I could just recall her name ... Isn't it funny how one can forget?

ANNIE: *(Nervous, meek)* Yes.

FRANCIS: Now let's see. Mary ... no, Margaret ... no ...

(ANNIE is trying to ignore her by looking for the cabinet)

FRANCIS: Lillian ... no, Louise, Harriet, no, Ida, Isobel, Georgette ...

ANNIE: FRANCIS!

FRANCIS: Yes ... you've got it!

(ANNIE has her back turned, is upset)

FRANCIS: *(As herself)* The cabinet is behind you. I'll assist you.

(Walks over)

ANNIE: *(Trying to regain composure)* I'm sorry, Francis, I ... I don't know what got into me, but I never thought you would ... I never expected you to recall ...

FRANCIS: *(After pouring two drinks, hands a glass to ANNIE)* Your Creme de Cacao. I haven't forgotten, Annie. Do you think 12 years really means anything? Do you think one can simply put experience after experience out of one's mind? How can you be so naive?

ANNIE: I thought we could start ... I thought all these years, all the changes could bring about a ... a fresh ... *(Staring)* ... a whole new beginning. *(Pause)* Francis, you must see what I mean!

(FRANCIS takes a cigarette)

ANNIE: Years do change people. There is growth! Maturity of course. I feel it myself. You must! It's there. I have changed. I don't believe you can dwell in some sort of personal museum. No, no! Francis, I am sure of it. Don't do this!

(FRANCIS offers her a cigarette)

ANNIE: No! I am here ... that's all you need ... nothing from the past ... just what I am now. You can ...

FRANCIS: *(laughs to herself)* Live with just that? And simply erase a decade of memory ... poof?! All gone ... just like that? *(Short pause)* The color of your hair has changed ... you're taller, of course ... not doe-like anymore. You used to refer to yourself as "knobknees." *(Laughs)* Whenever we came to a staircase I used to wait for a moment and then proceed behind you ... watching you work your way up the stairs ... somehow your thinking was just like the way you walked ... you would ... amble from one side to the next, and after a bit I became more than just entranced ... I felt I was responsible in case you fell or ... stopped thinking about what you were doing ... one side to the next, your dresses would sway with such an awkward rhythm, but you always made it ... and I was always out of breath ... from the worrying ...

DOC

Sharon Pollock

Place: Doc's house
Time: unspecified
Characters: Ev, 73; his daughter Catherine

Pollock's play revolves around Ev, a retired doctor of medicine, who is
about to have a hospital named after him. Throughout his life, Ev has
made many sacrifices for medicine, and there have been casualties
along the way. In fact, his mother may have committed suicide
because Ev ignored her; the letter in Ev's hand, at the beginning of
the scene, is perhaps his mother's suicide note. And Ev's wife Bob was
driven to drink and adultery by Ev's lack of sympathy for anything
other than medicine. Catherine has learned many hard lessons from
her mother and grandmother - especially that a woman should not
live her life vicariously through men.

Ev has suffered a heart attack. Catherine has traveled a long distance,
by airplane, to be at his side - not to witness the sod-breaking, as Ev
suggests, but to make peace with her father.

(Square brackets are used to indicate lines to be omitted in a two-
character scene.)

● ● ●

CATHERINE: ... It's me, Daddy.
EV: Katie?
[**KATIE:** When I was little, Daddy.]
CATHERINE: It's Catherine now, call me Catherine ... well ... aren't
you going to say anything?
EV: You're home.
CATHERINE: Ah-huh ... a hug, a big hug, Daddy, come on.
(CATHERINE and EV embrace)
Ooh.
EV: What.
CATHERINE: How long has it been?
EV: Be ah ....
CATHERINE: Four years, right? Medical convention in where? Van-
couver, right?

EV: That's right. Vancouver.

CATHERINE: Montreal, Toronto, Calgary, Van, where haven't we met, eh?

EV: Here.

CATHERINE: Yup. Not ... not met here.

(CATHERINE notices the envelope in EV's hand)

What're you doing with that?

EV: Oh - just goin' through things. Clearin' things out.

(CATHERINE, getting out a cigarette, turns away from EV)

[**BOB:** Katie's afraid of what she wrote.]

[**KATIE:** *(To CATHERINE)* Is that true?]

EV: Are you here for this hoopla tomorrow?

CATHERINE: Not really.

EV: There's gonna be speeches and more speeches. I lay the cornerstone, and dinner I think.

CATHERINE: Ah-huh.

EV: I got it all written down with the times.

CATHERINE: Ah-huh.

EV: I got it downstairs ... You wanna take a look? ... Not here for that, eh.

CATHERINE: No. I came home to see you.

EV: Pretty sad state of affairs when your own daughter's in town and can't attend a sod-turnin' in honor of her father.

CATHERINE: So I'll go, I'll be there.

EV: Coulda sent a telegram, saved the airfare.

CATHERINE: Christ Daddy, don't be so stupid.

EV: Sound like your mother.

CATHERINE: I learnt the four-letter words from you.

EV: Bullshit.

CATHERINE: I said I'd go, I said I'd be there. So. *(Pause)* I'm proud of you, Daddy.

EV: Did you know it was a write-in campaign?

CATHERINE: Oh?

EV: The niggers from Barker's Point, the mill workers from Marysville, they're the ones got this hospital named after me. Left to the politicians God knows what they'd have called it.

CATHERINE: Well, I'm proud.

EV: Some goddamn French name I suppose - what?

CATHERINE: Proud, you must be proud having the hospital named after you.

EV: The day I first started practice, that day I was proud. Was the day after you were born ... There was a scarlet fever epidemic that year, you remember?

CATHERINE: No Daddy.

EV: Somebody ... some couple came in, they were carryin' their

daughter, what was she? Two, maybe three? I took her in my arms ...
could see they'd left it too late. I remember that child. I passed her
back to her mother. Hold her tight, I said. Hold her tight 'til she goes
... Do you remember that woman holdin' that child in the hallway?

CATHERINE: No Daddy.

EV: No. That was your mother ... that was your mother.

[**BOB:** Blueberries, Katie.]

EV: You were just little then.

[**BOB:** Blueberries along the railway tracks, and every year we'd pick
them and sell them. I was the youngest, and Mama was always afraid
I'd get lost, but I never got lost.
(CATHERINE looks at BOB)
Not once.]
(Pause)

EV: What are you thinkin'?

CATHERINE: *(Looks away from BOB)* Nothing ... You've lost weight.

EV: Of course I lost. I damn near died. You didn't know that, did you.

CATHERINE: No. No, nobody told me.

EV: Well it was that goddamn heart man. It was him gave me a heart
attack.

CATHERINE: Really?

EV: What the hell's his name?

CATHERINE: Whose?

EV: The heart man's!

CATHERINE: I wouldn't know, Daddy.

EV: Demii - no, Demsky. I go to him, I tell him I been gettin' this pain
in my ticker, and he has me walkin' up and down this little set a stairs,
and runnin' on treadmills. Jesus Christ, I said to him, I'm not tryin'
out for a sports team, I'm here because I keep gettin' this pain in my
ticker! For Christ's sake, I said, put a stethoscope to my chest before
you kill me with these goddamn stairs!

CATHERINE: So how are you now?

EV: It would've served the bastard right if I'd died right there in his
office - do you remember how good Valma was with your mother?

CATHERINE: I remember.

EV: Every statutory holiday your mother's killin' herself or seein'
things crawlin' on the walls or some goddamn thing or other, and
Valma is like a rock, isn't that right?

CATHERINE: I guess so.

EV: So I come home from Demsky's, and I get the pain in my ticker and
I wait all night for it to go away, and long about four or 4:30, I phone
Valma. Valma, I say, I'm havin' a heart attack, Valma - and she drops
the phone nearly breakin' my eardrum and I can't phone out and I'm
damned if I'm gonna get in that car and die all alone on Charlotte
Street like that foolish Hazen Arbeton - If you were livin' in town, I'd

have phoned you.

CATHERINE: You couldn't if Valma dropped the phone, Daddy.

EV: I'd have phoned you first!

CATHERINE: Would you?

EV: Well if I'd known she was gonna drop that goddamn phone I would have.

CATHERINE: What about Robbie?

EV: Who?

CATHERINE: Your son - Robbie.

EV: I'm not senile, I know who the hell Robbie is, what about him?

CATHERINE: You could have phoned him.

EV: I couldn't phone anyone! I was connected to Valma and I couldn't get disconnected!

CATHERINE: Would you have phoned him if you could?

EV: He wouldn't be home.

CATHERINE: How do you know?

EV: He's never home.

CATHERINE: Do you see him much?

EV: How the hell could I if he's never home?

CATHERINE: Do you TRY to see him!

EV: Of course I try! Have you seen him, phoned him, been over to visit?

CATHERINE: For Christ's sake Daddy, I just got in.

EV: Do you write?

CATHERINE: To Robbie?

EV: Yes to Robbie! You sure as hell don't write to me!

CATHERINE: I don't have the time.

EV: Some people make time.

CATHERINE: Why don't you?

EV: I'm busy.

CATHERINE: So am I.

EV: Mn. *(Pause)* Does he ever write you?

CATHERINE: No.

EV: Do you wonder why?

CATHERINE: He's busy! Everyone's busy!

EV: Bullshit. It's that woman of his.

CATHERINE: It isn't.

EV: Paula.

CATHERINE: Who's Paula?

EV: She thinks we're all crazy.

CATHERINE: Well maybe we are, who in hell's Paula?

EV: His wife!

CATHERINE: You mean Corinne.

EV: What did I say?

CATHERINE: You said Paula.

EV: Well I meant Corinne! *(Pause)* Paula. Who the hell's Paula? *(Pause)*

[**BOB:** Pauline.]

EV: Pauline now, that was a friend of your mother's. Died a cancer, died in your room, and where did you sleep?

CATHERINE: In this room

EV: because

CATHERINE: the maid had left

EV: and your mother nursed Pauline right through to the end. Didn't touch a drop for three months.

[As CATHERINE turns away, she sees BOB]

[**BOB:** Not a drop for three months, Katie.]

(Pause)

EV: Best ... best office nurse ... I - ever had.

CATHERINE: Who, Mummy?

EV: Not Mummy, no. Valma. She ran that office like Hitler rollin' through Poland, and good with your mother -

CATHERINE: *(turns back to EV)* I know, 40 years like a rock.

EV: That's right, like a rock, but I call her with that heart attack, and she goes hysterical. I never saw that in her before. It was a surprise. It was a goddamn disappointment. She comes runnin' into the house and up the stairs and huffin' and puffin' and blue in the face and - I'm on the bathroom floor by this time. She sees that, and gets more hysterical. She's got to run next door - my phone not workin' bein' connected to her phone which she dropped breakin' my eardrum - and she phones the hospital. And then we sit - I lie, she sits - and we wait for the goddamn ambulance, her holdin' my hand and bawlin'.

CATHERINE: Poor Valma.

EV: Poor Valma be damned! If I'd had the strength I'd have killed her. I kept tellin' her two things, I said it over and over - one, you keep that Demsky away from me - and you know what she does?

CATHERINE: She is 67.

EV: I'm 73, you don't see me goin' hysterical! And I'm the one havin' the heart attack!

CATHERINE: Alright.

EV: You know the first thing I lay eyes on when I wake up in that hospital bed? Well, do you!

CATHERINE: No, I don't know, no.

EV: First thing I see is that goddamn Demsky hangin' over me like a vulture. Demsky who gave me the heart attack! ... Next death bed wish I make I sure as hell won't make it to Valma.

CATHERINE: Well ... it wasn't a real death bed wish, Daddy. You're still here.

EV: No thanks to her!

(Pause)

CATHERINE: So?

EV: So what?

CATHERINE: Jesus Daddy, so how are you now?

EV: I don't read minds, I'm not a mind-reader!

CATHERINE: How are you!

EV: I'm fine!

CATHERINE: Good.

EV: What?

CATHERINE: I said good. Great. I'm glad that you're fine.

EV: Got the nitro pills ... pop a coupla them. Slow down they say. Don't get excited, don't talk too fast, don't walk too fast, don't, don't, don't, just pop a pill.

CATHERINE: Is it hard?

EV: Is what hard?

CATHERINE: Is it hard to slow down?

EV: ... The nurses could always tell when I'd started my rounds. They could hear my heels hittin' the floor tiles, hear me a wing away.

THE FIGHTING DAYS

Wendy Lill

Place: on a train to Winnipeg
Time: 1910
Characters: Lily, 25; Francis, 18

The Fighting Days is based on the true story of Francis Beynon, journalist with the *Grain Growers' Guide*, author of the novel *Aleta Day*, supporter and critic of Nellie McClung.

In this (opening) scene of the play, Francis and her sister Lily are on a train from their prairie hometown to Lily's place in Winnipeg. Both girls have grown up on the patriarchal family farm, and both (but especially Francis) feel liberated by the recent death of their father. As the scene begins, Francis is "looking out the window, lost in thought"; Lily is crocheting.

LILY: Do you think Father's up there right now watching us?

FRANCIS: I never really believed in that part. Did you?

LILY: No, I guess not. Some things just sort of stick with you. He said he'd be joining Grandpa in heaven the day after he died, so there'd be no point in trying to put anything over on him. *(She smiles)* I remember you saying that if he was going to heaven, you didn't want to go there. That you'd rather go to hell.

FRANCIS: But I never really stood up to him. Had I been braver, Lily, I would have defied him.

LILY: You were braver than the rest of us. It was you Father went after. You seemed to bring out the worst in him.

FRANCIS: Why do you think that was?

LILY: Mother says it was your questions that made him angry. He thought they sprang from an "undisciplined spirit" ... whatever that means.

FRANCIS: You know when he used to ask "are you right with God"? What did you say?

LILY: I said "yes" every time and then he stopped bothering me.

FRANCIS: But how does one know whether they're RIGHT with God?

LILY: I don't know, Fanny.

FRANCIS: Do you believe deep in your heart that Methodists are the only ones with immortal souls?

LILY: Not any more. Not since I moved to the city.

FRANCIS: What happened then?

LILY: I guess I started to think ... bigger. I met people who believed in all sorts of things. Some of my friends are Presbyterians. Vernon, the young man I'm seeing at the newspaper, is an agnostic.

FRANCIS: An agnostic? I've never even heard of that church. What does he believe?

LILY: Well ... he believes ... well, he's not sure there really is a God ... he's just not sure.

FRANCIS: *(Concerned)* Oh.

LILY: But he's very nice, Fanny. He went to school in England. He reads a lot, just like you.

FRANCIS: If you like him, Lily, I'm sure I will.
(Silence)
Lily, what about the Catholics?

LILY: What about them?

FRANCIS: Are they all right too?

LILY: Yes, they're all right too.

FRANCIS: That's good. I always thought it was sad that Mrs. Sawatsky was going straight to hell after raising all those kids. Lily, what do you remember most about him?

LILY: "Serve the Lord with fear, with trembling kiss his feet, lest he be angry and you perish ... for his wrath is quickly kindled." There was always so much wrath.

FRANCIS: I'll always remember looking to see if his workboots were by the kitchen door. That meant he was in the house and I'd get that frightened feeling in my stomach. Lily, did you think he was ever going to die? I didn't. The horse died on its feet on the hottest day of the summer. Gippy and Rex crept off by themselves and died. I was scared that Mother would die in the yard with a load of wet laundry in her arms and that look on her face and I'd be left alone with him. I shouldn't have said that.

LILY: You can't help the way you feel. *(Squeezing her sister's hand)* Let's not talk about it any more. *(Pause)*

FRANCIS: Lily, does this mean I'm free now?

LILY: Free?

FRANCIS: Free. Free to sing in the house, push peas around on my plate, screw up my face, play cards, read books ...

LILY: *(Laughing)* All of those things! And Mother will be 60 miles away with Uncle George and not worrying over your soul any longer.

FRANCIS: Thank heavens!

LILY: I'm going to take care of you now. We'll get a nice bright room in the West End with elm trees out front. We'll go to picture shows and tea rooms and libraries.

FRANCIS: Libraries!

LILY: And you can meet my newspaper friends and join my suffrage club.

FRANCIS: Your what?

LILY: My suffrage club. Oh, you'll learn about that soon enough.

FRANCIS: *(Looking doubtful)* Do you think I'll fit in?

LILY: Of course you will. You're going to love the city!

FRANCIS: Do you think so?

LILY: *(Hugging her)* I do. And furthermore, the city will love you! Oh Fanny, you're a brick!

THE FIGHTING DAYS

Wendy Lill

Place: office of *The Rural Review*, a farm newspaper published in
  Winnipeg
Time: 1912 or 1913
Characters: Francis, George McNair

Shortly after arriving in Winnipeg, Francis lands a job writing for the
  women's page of *The Rural Review*. Influenced by Nellie McClung,
  who is a friend of Francis' sister Lily, she has transformed the
  women's page into a forum for women's suffrage. Francis' editor
  George McNair views this transformation with wry amusement. One
  senses that he tolerates Francis' opinions because he is in love with
  her; he will later ask her to marry him.

MCNAIR: Let's see what you've got on your page this week.
  (He pulls the page out of the typewriter and begins to read aloud)
  "We have too long been contented with the kind of motherhood
  that can turn its back on mere children toiling incredible hours in
  factories making bullets and ammunition and uniforms for some
  faraway war and yet calmly say, `Thank God it's not my children.'
  What we need now is a new spirit of national motherhood." And
  someone who can write shorter sentences. National motherhood.
  National motherhood? You make it sound like the railway, Miss
  Beynon.
FRANCIS: *(Deflated)* I quite liked that expression.
MCNAIR: Is it yours?
FRANCIS: Well ...
MCNAIR: It sounds like something off of Mrs. McClung's bat. You
  seem to have an opinion about everything lately. National mother-
  hood, intemperate husbands, the German war machine, the profes-
  sion of parenthood, the Boy Scout movement, and suffrage ad
  nauseum. But I find myself wondering ... what happened to your
  columns on mothers and babies, ginger snaps and peonies? What

about the little crocheted sweaters for the wee ones. Hmmmm? What about those things? They're important, too.

FRANCIS: Do you think they are more important than freedom from cruel husbands and fathers, from hypocritical ministers, from war-mongering politicians?

MCNAIR: Oh, don't bludgeon me with adjectives. Just say what you mean.

FRANCIS: I'm sorry.

MCNAIR: Unfortunately, the things you mention will always be with us. Scotch broth and shortbread and a garden full of bluebells make them a bit more tolerable. My mother knew that. She would never have bothered herself with voting and chasing men out of bars.

FRANCIS: But was she happy?

MCNAIR: Happy? I don't know. She seemed content. She smiled a lot.

FRANCIS: You mean she just put up with it.

MCNAIR: Perhaps. But the point is, she had enough to do in the home. You'll be wise to keep that in mind.

FRANCIS: If you think that women belong in the home, why did you hire me?

MCNAIR: I had no choice. What self-respecting man would want to write about "women's things"? Unfortunately, you don't seem interested in writing about them either.

FRANCIS: Mr. McNair, are you not finding my work satisfactory?

MCNAIR: Did I say that?

FRANCIS: You imply that.

MCNAIR: I do not. I think that the suffrage question is ... interesting, but you take it much too far. Mrs. McClung need only pen one of her silly little verses and it somehow finds its way into your editorials.

FRANCIS: Mrs. McClung is at the forefront of the suffrage cause.

MCNAIR: She is a dilettante and a debutante. And a hypocrite. She's an upper class snob who wouldn't have given my poor mother the time of day.

FRANCIS: That's not true. Nellie McCLung is fighting for the vote for women.

MCNAIR: For women who don't need the vote. For women who've got something better than the vote! Influence! And furthermore, the proper lineage!

FRANCIS: No!

MCNAIR: No? Then tell me why your suffrage club list is full of names like Stewart, Titheradge, Ward, Galbraith, Gordon, and not ... Lewycky, Schapansky and Swartz?

FRANCIS: Well, maybe their husbands won't let them come.

MCNAIR: They're not there because your suffrage club doesn't want them there. Neither do they want them living next to them on Chestnut Street nor their children sitting beside theirs at school.

FRANCIS: Mr. McNair, I believe in democracy for ALL women. I do!

MCNAIR: Then you're in the minority. Isobel Graham has gone on record saying she's afraid the entire western hemisphere is sinking under the weight of the immigrants.

FRANCIS: Isobel has ... a blind spot.

MCNAIR: And Laura McLaughlin, another one of your leading lights, is heading up the fight to eliminate any foreign language in the schoolyard.

FRANCIS: That's because Laura thinks it's important that newcomers learn English.

MCNAIR: That's because she hates the very idea of them.

FRANCIS: I admit there are some members who don't feel comfortable with all the strangers in our midst, but that will change. It takes time to alter attitudes. It takes time to remove the walls of class and privilege and ethnic differences that ...

MCNAIR: Oh, don't start that again! The fact is the suffragists are an exclusive club. And you'd do well to stay away from them.

FRANCIS: I find it curious how you suddenly spring to the defense of foreign women. Because in the year that I've known you, you have never shown interest in ANY women having the vote, whether their name was Gordon or Schapansky! I'm beginning to think that you just enjoy muddying the waters!

MCNAIR: *(Winking)* I enjoy arguing with you. You argue like a man!

FRANCIS: Well, I am not.

MCNAIR: And I'm glad you're not.

FRANCIS: *(Flustered)* I believe in the vote for women, all women, and I am going to keep fighting for it.

MCNAIR: Now don't get so flustered. It's not that important, is it?

FRANCIS: Mr. McNair, let me try to explain something to you. When I was a child, on the farm, I was constantly asking questions. Does God ever change his mind? Why was he angry all the time? Why couldn't I talk to the Polish children on the next farm? Why didn't my father help them out like the other neighbors? But nobody wanted to answer my questions. There seemed to be a secret fraternity at work that I didn't understand. My father and the Methodist minister and later my teachers thrashed and sermonized and ridiculed me until my spirit shrank and I began to doubt my very worth.

MCNAIR: It doesn't seem to have been a lasting affliction. You seem to have quite an unswerving confidence.

FRANCIS: Well, I don't. I still cower at the voice of authority. Even now, I tense up as you, my editor, come into the room. Do you understand what I'm talking about?

MCNAIR: Yes, I think so, but I'm not sure what it has to do with suffrage.

FRANCIS: Oh, but it's all connected! When I came to the city, I met women fighting for the freedom to think and worship and question for themselves. Women who challenge authority ... who look it right in the eye and say, prove you're worthy of respect! I felt like I'd been let out of prison. I felt like a great gleam of sunlight had broken through the fog. And I didn't feel alone any more!

MCNAIR: You're a funny one. You remind me of those little birds I found trapped in the house when I was a child. My mother would make me catch them and let them go free outside. And whenever I caught them, I could feel their little hearts beating in my hand, and I wanted to tell them not to be afraid, that I wasn't going to hurt them. You're like one of those little birds. Miss Beynon, I understand you live alone since your sister married. Perhaps you might be needing someone to look in on you once in a while.

FRANCIS: I would like that very much.

MCNAIR: Good, then. I will do that. It's time you associated with someone who still holds womanhood sacred.

FRANCIS: No! I don't need anyone to hold womanhood sacred. I hold womanhood sacred myself. I do!

MCNAIR: Well, you hold it at quite a distance. It might help your cause if you applied some rouge to your cheeks occasionally. Good day, Miss Beynon, I'll let you get back to national motherhood.

HEROES

Ken Mitchell

Place: waiting room of the Chief's office, downtown New York
Time: 3:30 p.m.; year unspecified; play first produced in 1975
Characters: the Lone Ranger, Superman

The Chief, who has all the characteristics of a god in this lonely universe
populated by super-heroes, has summoned the Lone Ranger and
Superman to his office. Neither super-hero knows why the meeting
has been called, but it is clear that each is afraid his popularity is
waning. In fact, they are being demoted. Lois Lane and Tonto will be
the protagonists from now on; Superman and the Lone Ranger will
be reduced to playing the role of sidekicks.

*The LONE RANGER enters, looking tense and high-strung. He glances around
quickly, looking for an ambush. There is only SUPERMAN.*
RANGER: *(Touching his hat)* Afternoon.
   *(SUPERMAN ignores him, except for one flick of the eyes. RANGER, almost
   casually, checks his revolver, and sits down cautiously on the opposite side
   of the Chief's door. He suddenly seems very tired, tilts his hat back. He lifts
   his mask - like spectacles - to rub his eyes. He sees SUPERMAN look at him,
   and quickly lowers the mask again. They sit silently. RANGER speaks
   finally)*
RANGER: It is not easy to stable a horse in downtown New York.
SUPERMAN: I suppose not.
RANGER: Take my advice.
SUPERMAN: Hm?
RANGER: Don't ever try it. Finally had to leave him in a parking lot.
   (Defensively) Well, I couldn't just tie him to a parking meter, could I?
SUPERMAN: You can't leave him by himself?
RANGER: Certainly not.
SUPERMAN: Kinda stupid ,is he?
RANGER: *(Bristling)* Silver is not stupid!
SUPERMAN: A bit - ornery?
RANGER: Do you mind if we change the subject?
SUPERMAN: Okay, okay! *(Pause)* So - you're in the horse business,
   huh?
RANGER: No, I am not in the "horse business."

SUPERMAN: What's with the weird costume, then?
(RANGER looks at his clothes, then SUPERMAN's, rather pointedly. He does not reply)
Cows?
RANGER: No.
SUPERMAN: Sheep?
RANGER: No!
SUPERMAN: *(Pause)* Pigs?
RANGER: No!
SUPERMAN: Sor-r-r-ry! *(Pause)* It's a bit - passé, isn't it? The boots and everything.
RANGER: All sorts of people wear clothes like this.
(RANGER, getting irritated, snatches a magazine and snaps through a few pages. He is trying to think of a comeback)
May I ask what you're doing here?
SUPERMAN: Here?
RANGER: In this office.
SUPERMAN: *(Curtly)* Business.
RANGER: What kind of business?
SUPERMAN: *(Long pause)* What's the mask all about?
RANGER: Huh?
SUPERMAN: *(Very clearly)* Mask?
RANGER: Are you trying to say you don't know?
SUPERMAN: *(Pretending to think)* Batman!
RANGER: *(Through clenched teeth)* Are you here on official business?
SUPERMAN: *(Enjoying himself)* Who wants to know?
RANGER: The Lone Ranger wants to know!
SUPERMAN: *(Pause)* Who?
RANGER: Lone Ranger! Lone Ranger! What the - heck do you think this mask is for?
SUPERMAN: Oh, I dunno - you see a lotta funny sights downtown these days.
(RANGER leaps to his feet, snatches a couple of cartridges from his gun belt, pushes them in SUPERMAN's face)
RANGER: Look! Look at these!
SUPERMAN: *(Non-committal)* Interesting.
RANGER: Interesting? They're solid silver!
SUPERMAN: Some kind of dum-dums, are they?
RANGER: They're my own special bullets!
SUPERMAN: But why - silver?
RANGER: *(Taken by surprise)* Well, it's a kind of - trademark.
SUPERMAN: Oh. *(Pause)* Oh! A horse called Silver! That mask! You're...
RANGER: *(With some satisfaction)* The Lone Ranger.
SUPERMAN: Right! A fiery horse with the speed of ...
RANGER: Light!

SUPERMAN: Yeah. A cloud of dust and a hearty ... *(Looks slyly at RANGER)* ... Giddy-ap?

RANGER: *(Frostily)* Hi-yo Silver, away!

SUPERMAN: Yeah, I remember now. *(Shakes his head)* Man, that's a long time!

RANGER: What?

SUPERMAN: That musta been, what? Fifteen, 20 years ...?

RANGER: For your information, I've spent the last three weeks chasing a gang of desperate outlaws!

SUPERMAN: Train-robbers?

RANGER: *(Pause)* Dope peddlers.

SUPERMAN: You don't say? *(Friendlier)* Where's your, um, buddy?

RANGER: *(With the proper dignity)* I ride alone.

SUPERMAN: Oh, come on! Otto or whatever his ...

RANGER: His name is Tonto.

SUPERMAN: Otto. Tonto. Pronto.

RANGER: And he is not my "buddy." He is my - faithful Indian companion.

SUPERMAN: *(Laughs)* He's what?

RANGER: You wouldn't understand. Easterners never do.

SUPERMAN: Whuddaya mean - Easterner?

RANGER: *(Not above sarcasm himself)* From - the - East.

SUPERMAN: Listen, pal. This might be a little hard for you to follow, but I've got a lot of territory to cover. *(Dramatic pause)* I serve the world!

RANGER: The world?

SUPERMAN: Yeah - the world.
(Gestures a globe)
You know?

RANGER: *(Suspiciously)* You sound like one of those anarchists.

SUPERMAN: *(Incredulous)* What?

RANGER: You are implying there's something wrong with the good old U.S. of A., right?

SUPERMAN: Jesus. How long have you been out in Texas, anyway?

RANGER: Arizona.

SUPERMAN: Arizona.

RANGER: *(Pause, with steely intent)* I believe we were discussing you.

SUPERMAN: Look, pal! I'm not wearing mask! I got nothing to hide.

RANGER: I suppose that - red cape is supposed to represent something, is it?

SUPERMAN: Represent?

RANGER: *(Just getting warmed up)* Are you domiciled in this land of liberty and enterprise?

SUPERMAN: Huh?

RANGER: Do you live here?

SUPERMAN: Yeah, in a way.

RANGER: *(Grimly)* Now you are evading my questions!

SUPERMAN: No, I'm not! I just - well, I stay with a friend of mine. Clark Kent!

RANGER: You stay with a male friend?

SUPERMAN: Sort of. Clark is a reporter for ...

RANGER: Male - right?

SUPERMAN: Yes!

RANGER: And this little - home of yours is in the East, right?

SUPERMAN: Jesus Christ! Is all this ... ?

RANGER: Right?

SUPERMAN: - relevant?

RANGER: *(Pause)* I could tell you were a fruit, the minute I laid eyes on that outfit.

(SUPERMAN looks at his costume in surprise)

They'd laugh you out of every town west of the Mississippi.

SUPERMAN: They would not!

RANGER: Try it and see.

SUPERMAN: I been west of the Mississippi hundreds of times. Thousands of times!

RANGER: Did you take your - friend along? Clark Kent?

SUPERMAN: Yes. No! He has to stay in - Metropolis.

RANGER: Metropolis, eh?

SUPERMAN: He works there.

RANGER: I never heard of it.

SUPERMAN: *(Trying hard)* You wouldn't have.

RANGER: *(Pause)* Still, I will say it's - colorful.

SUPERMAN: What?

RANGER: Well, that bikini. The cape. The monogrammed shirt ...

SUPERMAN: Monog ...! That's my symbol!

RANGER: "S" for symbol, I suppose.

SUPERMAN: *(Dangerously quiet)* Do you know that with a single breath, I could blow you right through that wall?

RANGER: Well, you've been doing your darnedest for 10 minutes now.

SUPERMAN: Do you realize that one blow from this - fist of steel could send you into orbit around the moon?

RANGER: *(Unimpressed)* A hazard I could learn to live with.

SUPERMAN: You're starting to - piss - me - off, fella!

RANGER: *(Satisfied with his victory, stands up to ease the tension)* Have you been waiting here long?

(SUPERMAN refuses to answer)

(Cajoling) Aw, come on. There's no point in sulking. If we gotta water at the same trough, we might as well pretend to be neighborly.

SUPERMAN: Do you mind laying off the hillbilly metaphors?

RANGER: Pardon?

SUPERMAN: Save it for your - fans!

RANGER: Suit yourself. I was only trying to pass the time of day.

SUPERMAN: *(Pause)* Fifteen minutes!

RANGER: Pardon?

SUPERMAN: I was waiting - 15 minutes!
  (Pause)

RANGER: What did you mean about my fans?

SUPERMAN: Fans?

RANGER: You said - save it for my fans.

SUPERMAN: *(Bored)* Did I?*(Pause. The telephone behind the Chief's door
  rings three times. SUPERMAN listens intently. RANGER tries to hear, too,
  but can't. SUPERMAN finally shakes his head in disgust)*
  So where's your "faithful Indian companion"?

RANGER: Oh, he's out at the silver mine. He can't stand the East.
  Couldn't drag him here with a herd of mustangs.

SUPERMAN: Did you say silver mine?

RANGER: Yeah.

SUPERMAN: You guys own a silver mine?

RANGER: Yeah. That's where these come from.

SUPERMAN: You mean that's all you do with it?

RANGER: Do with what?

SUPERMAN: Man, do you know how much silver is worth these days?
  (This sends RANGER off into one of his standard speeches)

RANGER: Oh, yes! I do know its worth. In fact, that material value
  which you attach to it is what we seek to destroy - by constantly
  employing these shining bullets as weapons in the fight for justice,
  and for decency, and for freedom. *(Stabbing the air)* By eradicating the
  root of all evil from existence, we will preserve our founders' heritage
  and ...

SUPERMAN: You don't have to tell me, pal. Ever since I got to this
  planet, it's been fight, fight, fight - just to keep a little law and order.

RANGER: *(Pleasantly surprised)* You mean - you too are engaged in the
  eternal battle against evil and perversion?

SUPERMAN: *(Modestly)* In my own little way.

RANGER: There aren't many of us left these days.

SUPERMAN: It gets lonely sometimes.

RANGER: *(Pause, checks his watch)* Hope that parking lot attendant is
  reliable.

SUPERMAN: I wouldn't trust one with a stale sandwich.

RANGER: *(Alarmed)* Maybe I better go check ...!

SUPERMAN: Oh come on. Where's he going to go with a horse?

RANGER: *(Agrees)* Yeah. *(Pause, a bit puzzled)* That's strange about the
  fans.

SUPERMAN: What is?

RANGER: That's what he said, too. "Save it for your fans."

SUPERMAN: Who?

(RANGER looks around cautiously, flicks his thumb at the Chief's door)

RANGER: Him.

SUPERMAN: He invited you here?

RANGER: Yes.

SUPERMAN: All the way from Texas?

RANGER: Arizona. He telephoned.

(SUPERMAN seems shaken by this; put out, distracted)

What is it?

SUPERMAN: Oh, nothing. Nothing. *(Pause, suddenly)* You ever get - premonitions?

RANGER: *(Startled himself)* Premonitions? What about?

SUPERMAN: Well, I dunno. *(Pause)* Had a kinda funny thing happen on the way over here - from Metropolis.

RANGER: Like what?

SUPERMAN: I guess it was over - Baltimore - I happened to look down, and there was this house on fire. In the suburbs. There were all these people, a family, screaming from the windows, so I swooped down to help.

RANGER: *(Too politely, not believing a word)* Oh?

SUPERMAN: There was a little baby! And an old guy, must have been 80! They wouldn't have stood a chance!

RANGER: I suppose not. *(Long pause)* What exactly do you mean, you swooped down?

SUPERMAN: Well I was in a rush, see - flying over and ...

RANGER: You were flying over.

SUPERMAN: Yeah, and all this smoke curling up. Man, I flew right through it.

RANGER: Let me get this straight. You were flying along in this balloon, or airplane or whatever, and you just happened to look down and see ...

SUPERMAN: No, no! I was flying - all by myself!

(RANGER begins flapping his arms like a bird, and caws like a crow)

You see I've had the power of flight since ... *(Turns to RANGER)* Okay, knock it off, hayseed! *(SUPERMAN turning away)* Anyway, when I - landed, they - all started to laugh. They said to - kiss off. It was a big joke! What are you grinning at?

RANGER: Well - flying! That's a big far-fetched, isn't it?

SUPERMAN: No more than those goddamn silver bullets!

RANGER: Eh?

SUPERMAN: I don't expect some dumb cowboy to know this, but I - am Superman!

RANGER: *(Suppressing a laugh)* Who?

SUPERMAN: Superman!

(RANGER's laugh runs down in the silence)

RANGER: All right - "Superman," what are you doing in here? In my Chief's office?

SUPERMAN: Your Chief's office?

RANGER: Yes.

SUPERMAN: Say, how do you earn your money, anyway?

RANGER: Well, I - don't. I mean, Tonto looks after that side of things. *(Pause)* Probably makes a few bucks selling beadwork and - stuff.

SUPERMAN: Beadwork, huh?

RANGER: Sure! There's good money in - well, how do you make money? Put on some kind of - flying circus?

SUPERMAN: Clark gets a good salary at the Daily Planet. It keeps us in groceries.

HOSANNA
Michel Tremblay

Place: Hosanna's furnished bachelor apartment on Plaza Saint-Hubert, Montreal

Time: late evening in October; year unspecified; the play was written in 1973

Characters: Hosanna (Claude); Cuirette

If success in transvestism is achieved by outdoing one's colleagues in the field of social adroitness, then Hosanna has been a successful transvestite. Originally from a small town in Quebec, she (which is the pronoun Tremblay uses) discovered her sexual preference early in life and decided to move to Montreal where she soon "got ahead in this town by being a bitch." Evidence of her success is that she has won the heart of Cuirette, a biker who, at one time, set the transvestite community ablaze but who is now considered a little old and overweight.

Two months ago Sandra, a local club owner and transvestite, announced that the theme of her annual Halloween bash would be Famous Women in History. At that instant, everyone knew who Hosanna would dress up as—her idol Elizabeth Taylor, in the role of Cleopatra.

The night of the party arrived. Hosanna had planned to make her entrance with no less fanfare than when Taylor/Cleopatra entered Rome in the movie, "borne aloft in her chair," admired by thousands of extras. When Hosanna arrived at the party, however, she found, to her dismay, that everyone else had dressed up as Taylor/Cleopatra and, more to her dismay, that everyone looked better than she. At first, Hosanna tried to take the rather tasteless joke in good humor, but she eventually lost control, hurried outside, jumped into a cab, and came home.

● ● ●

HOSANNA comes in very slowly, making no noise. She stands in the dark for a very long time, without moving. We hear her breathing, as if she were drinking the air of her apartment.

She can barely be seen in the flashing light of the neon sign. She should give the appearance of a bundle of rags that is somehow standing up.

HOSANNA: I knew I shouldn't have gone. I knew it ... I knew it ...

(She goes over to the urn-lamp and lights it. HOSANNA is a transvestite dressed up as Elizabeth Taylor playing "Cleopatra," but infinitely more cheap. A Cleopatra-of-the-streets. Her dress is in wine-red lace, heavily decorated in gold lace "in the style of the times." The wig is "real hair." Her sandals come directly from Park Avenue (Montreal), and the generous portion of jewels, necklaces, chains, rings, pins, and the cobra headpiece that HOSANNA-Cleopatra is wearing, and the serpents entwined around her arms, all come from any or several of the five- & 10-cent stores, or the "jewelry" shops that line la rue Sainte-Catherine between Amherst and Saint-Laurent. But despite this grotesque get-up, Claude-HOSANNA-Cleopatra should not appear "funny." She is a cheap transvestite, touching and sad, exasperating in her self-exaltation)

(HOSANNA stands for some time next to the urn-lamp. She looks in the mirror over the vanity table)

HOSANNA: I knew it. I knew it ... I should never have gone in there.
(She approaches the mirror and looks at herself, long and hard, from head to toe. She looks at herself as one transvestite looks at another. She starts trembling slightly)

(She grabs the bottle of perfume, douses her hands with the stuff, vigorously rubs them together, then turns toward the bed-sofa)

(There, sitting straight up, she begins to cry. With great difficulty at first, then more and more openly. She never puts her hands to her face, she doesn't budge, always sitting very straight, leaning forward ever so slightly)

HOSANNA: Stupid bitch! Cheap stupid bitch! Stupide, stupide, stupide...

(She calms down, then goes back to the mirror)

That's right, HOSANNA. While you're at it, get your face all streaked. Three hours of work. Half a pound of sequins! You get one of those in your eyes, you'll have plenty to cry about. Three hours of work! You stupid bitch.

(Silence)

A whole lifetime, a whole lifetime of preparation and look where it's got you. Congratulations! Congratulations on your terrific success!
(The roar of an old motorcycle is heard arriving outside the house)

Your prince has come, Hosanna. Time to shed these crimson robes!
(She takes off her gloves and tries to unhook the dress, but without success)

Shit! I forgot there were hooks. I'm going to get stuck in this thing, I just know it.

(A burst of laughter is heard on the stairway. A door slams, and CUIRETTE, in all his splendor, makes his entrance. Of CUIRETTE one would be inclined to say that he is an "old stud." As for the stud, only the costume remains. He is a stud grown old and fat, his leather jacket, once tight and provocative, has been too small for a long time. His old jeans are bulging more with fat than muscles. But as a stud, CUIRETTE has retained his arrogance and easy self-assurance, all of which makes him rather ridiculous sometimes)

CUIRETTE: "Hosanna, Hosanna, Hosanna, Ho! Hosanna, Hosanna, Hosanna, Ho!" Holy shit, what a laugh! I never laughed so hard in my life.

(He sees HOSANNA)

Well, what do you know, she's back! The Queen of the Nile is already on her throne! Hey, your taxi-driver must have been scared shitless, the way he was moving. I bet he just opened the door and dumped you out, like a bag of dirty laundry, eh? I tried to keep up with you, but he was moving so fast, and I was laughing so hard, I couldn't even steer. You know where I wound up? In the middle of Parc Lafontaine. It's not exactly on the way, but what could I do, eh, that's where the bike wanted to take me. Hey, Hosanna, it's been years since I was through there. And you know what those bastards have done? They've put lights up all over the place. It's lit up, bright as day, the whole park. Looks like shit ... Jesus Christ, it stinks in here! How many times I gotta tell you, the place smells like a two-bit whore house!

HOSANNA: You ... what do you know about whores?

CUIRETTE: Smells like a fuckin' perfume factory ...

HOSANNA: I said what do you know about whores? Did you ever get close enough to smell one?

CUIRETTE: Big Pauline-de-Joliette smelled like that. I dumped her, remember? Never went near her again. She made me want to puke.

HOSANNA: Poor baby. She must have cried her eyes out for a whole 30 seconds. By the way, what was her real name? Wasn't it Paul?

CUIRETTE: They're everywhere, Hosanna, everywhere. There isn't one lousy corner that's not lit up. How can you get any action in a place like that, eh? Christ, they even put in a zoo for the kids!

HOSANNA: It's been there for 15 years.

CUIRETTE: And a theater, too ... I drove right up to it on my bike ... All lit up, just like the rest. Lights everywhere. Jesus, you can't even get a decent blowjob anymore. Not a corner left in the park, Hosanna. I tell you, everything's changed. To get a good blowjob these days, you gotta find yourself a two-bit whore in a cheap perfume factory.

(He laughs)

HOSANNA: Okay, Cuirette, you've had a lot to drink tonight, and I think we'd better go to bed. When you can't even remember there's a zoo and a theater in the Parc Lafontaine, it's time to go to bed. We can talk about your perfume in the morning, if you like. Right now your two-bit whore has had about all that she can take.

CUIRETTE: Smells like somebody died in here.

(He laughs)

Hey, you know, when my Uncle Gratien kicked the bucket, the funeral parlor stunk like this. I remember my Aunt Germaine climbing into the casket screaming, "Don't leave me, Gratien, don't leave me!"

HOSANNA: I know, I know, and the lid of the coffin fell on her head; you've only told me 300 times. Three hundred times you've told me that story.

CUIRETTE: You don't think it's funny? Pow! Right on the head. And then you know what she says? "Oh yes, dear, yes, if you want me to follow you, I will. I'm coming with you, Gratien, I'm coming!" Christ, that was funny! And your room, Hosanna, reminds me of my Uncle Gratien's funeral, and my Aunt Germaine. That's why I'm talking about it.

HOSANNA: It's also because you've got nothing else to say ...

CUIRETTE: I said to myself: "Cuirette, my friend, they've built a theater on the very spot you made your debut." ... That's not bad, eh? ... not bad at all ...

HOSANNA: Ouais, and one day they're going to tear down the La Scala Theater, which is where you're going to end up, and they're going to build a park in its place ... A nice big park with lots and lots of toilets ... le Parc Raymond-Cuirette!

CUIRETTE: Goddamn lights, they're everywhere. They've ruined it, Hosanna, they've ruined my beautiful park. I started busting streetlights, but then I stopped 'cause they were the old ones, and the old ones look kind'a nice. You can't bust the new ones, they're too high. It looks like a baseball field, for Chrissake!

HOSANNA: Too bad it wasn't that bright when I met you, hein?

CUIRETTE: Hey, did you check out the taxi-driver? Whose type was he, yours or mine?

HOSANNA: Fat chance he'd be yours, Cuirette. Taxi-drivers dressed as women aren't that easy to come by. Even on Hallowe'en.

CUIRETTE: Some of them are women ...

HOSANNA: Real ones, yes, I know, stupid! It's not the first time in my life I've taken a taxi.

CUIRETTE: Yeah, but never that fast. Man, I've never seen you in such a flap.

HOSANNA: I wasn't in a flap.

CUIRETTE: You want to bet?

HOSANNA: I wasn't in a flap, stupid!

CUIRETTE: Sure, you kept your dignity 'til you got to the door. But as soon as you were out of sight you tore down those stairs like a bat out of hell. And this time you weren't too choosy about whose taxi you got into, eh? You didn't stand there wiggling your ass and giving them the eye, did you? No, you grabbed the first one that came along and you jumped in before the poor bastard knew what was happening. All he saw was a flash of red rags and scrap metal falling into his back seat, and someone screaming, "Get me out of here, get me out of here. I'll tell you where I'm going in a minute."

(HOSANNA goes up to CUIRETTE and turns her back to him)

HOSANNA: Will you unhook my dress?

CUIRETTE: If it takes as long to get out of it as it did to get in you may as well leave it on 'til next Hallowe'en.

HOSANNA: Listen, smarty-pants, if you don't want to do it, just say so and I'll do it myself ... I can do it myself, you know, if you don't want to help me.

CUIRETTE: No, no, I'll do it ...

(The phone rings. CUIRETTE grabs it before undoing even one hook)

Hello? ... *(Disappointed)* ... Oh ... yeah ... *(To HOSANNA)* ...it's for you...

HOSANNA: At this hour? Who is it?

CUIRETTE: I don't know ... I don't recognize her voice ...

HOSANNA: It's a woman?

CUIRETTE: I doubt it, but whoever she is, I don't know her.

(He starts laughing)

Well, here, see for yourself.

(HOSANNA takes the receiver)

HOSANNA: Oui, allo ...

(She stands fixed for a moment, then slams down the receiver and throws the phone on the floor.)

CUIRETTE: So, did you know her?

HOSANNA: Fat bitch!

CUIRETTE: Listen, baby, I've already told you. I'm not one of the girls.

HOSANNA: I wasn't talking to you ... You're not so important that I talk to you ALL the time. You're not THAT important! Besides, in that idiot outfit you look so little like a man, if anyone heard me calling you a bitch they'd take you for a lesbian!

CUIRETTE: Yeah. Well, I'm no lesbian, and I can prove it.

HOSANNA: You? You couldn't prove a goddamn thing. You don't got what it takes.

CUIRETTE: You want the proof, Hosanna?

HOSANNA: No thanks. I've swallowed enough for one night!

CUIRETTE: You're too much, you know that? Swallowed enough for one night. You really know how to dish it out, don't you? I'll bet your customers really lap it up when you talk like that.

HOSANNA: Ah, oui ... me, I'm the funniest hairdresser in town ...

(HOSANNA picks up the telephone, hesitates before putting it in place, then does so)

And I'm very, very popular with the Jewish ladies because I don't singe their hair ... Funny and clever! The secret of my success.

CUIRETTE: Does my Queen-of-the-Nile hairdresser still want to get unhooked?

(The telephone rings again, and HOSANNA grabs it right away)

HOSANNA: Go shit yourself, Sandra! Go shit yourself, you dried-up cunt!

(She hangs up)

THE IMPROMPTU OF OUTREMENT

Michel Tremblay

Place: the living room of a bourgeois home in Outrement, Quebec
Time: 1980
Characters: Yvette, Lucille

Every year, on Lucille's birthday, the four Beaugrand sisters return to
the family home (now occupied by Lucille and Yvette but owned by
the eldest sister Fernande) for a party. But the celebration routinely
turns into a series of arguments, with sister pitted against sister.
Fernande, bringer of the dainty birthday cakes, is at 50 the eldest
sister, a closet writer who prides herself on her elitism. Yvette—she
of the beautiful voice—is 46. Lorraine, who was once a remarkable
pianist, is now 43 and married to an Italian gardener from the wrong
side of town. Lucille is, at 40, unmarried.

As the scene begins, Yvette is listening to a recording of "Dido and
Aeneas" by Purcell. The aria "Remember Me," sung by Tatiana
Troyanas, is just ending. Lucille, who has been knitting in the same
room, gets up and shuts off the record player.

YVETTE: It's not over!
LUCILLE: I know.
YVETTE: There's still the chorus.
LUCILLE: I know there's still the chorus, it's the 10th time we've heard
it today! But I'm stopping it now, because if I let her die to the bitter
end, you'll only want to play it again! Dido will start to pine again,

Aeneas will come cooing in again, prancing like a gazelle, Dido will collapse in a swoon again, Aeneas will leave again, Dido will sing "Remember Me" again, and I will climb the walls or tear the wallpaper to shreds.

YVETTE: There's no wallpaper in here!

LUCILLE: There is in your bedroom. How would you like to go to sleep tonight in a room devastated by the sister you drove insane?

YVETTE: Of course, I wouldn't ...

LUCILLE: Then put Tatiana Troyanos back in her jacket and we'll play something else ...

YVETTE: *(Sarcastically)* Something Quebecois ...

(LUCILLE looks at YVETTE and shrugs her shoulders)

LUCILLE: You can play your Faure songs if you like, or even your Erna Sack, who howls like a cat in heat, over three generations of static, scratches and greasy fingerprints! Anything but "Remember Me!"

YVETTE: You have no sensitivity ...

LUCILLE: Licking your wounds while you listen to someone die 12 times a day, I don't call that sensitivity ...

YVETTE: No, you call it sentimentality, you've told me a hundred times.

LUCILLE: Right, so why bring it up again ...

YVETTE: And what is this about licking my wounds? As if I had any to lick!

(They look at one another for a moment. LUCILLE picks up her knitting again)

LUCILLE: No, I suppose you just "happened" to play "Remember Me" all these years. First, it was Kirsten Flagstad, then Janet Baker, and now it's Tatiana Troyanos ... Generations of singers pass, but "Remember Me" is not forgotten!

(Silence)

Why is that? Why not something else? Something light, uplifting? A happy ending instead of a stupid death ...

(YVETTE picks up her cup of tea, which has been sitting on a side table, getting cold)

YVETTE: The tea is cold.

(LUCILLE laughs)

Okay, now what did I say?

LUCILLE: "The tea is cold." That was enough ... It reminds me of Mother ... Whenever the time came for explanations, or the moment to finally say something important, invariably she would trot out one of those pearls which you have inherited: "The tea is cold!" or: "Oh dear, the clock is fast!" or: "Goodness me, I'm late!" All to avoid a discussion. Our mother was the epitome of empty words.

(She laughs)

You remember when Father died in her arms, cursing her, showering her with insults, almost spitting in her face, and she turned to us and said: "The terrible thing with cancer is that, near the end, we have to remove our dentures."

YVETTE: Yes, and you laughed, like the heartless thing you were.

LUCILLE: That's right, heartless ...

(Silence)

Given the choice between a heart and a sense of humor ...

YVETTE: More empty words ...

LUCILLE: Fair enough, that makes it one-all!

(YVETTE begins to flip nervously through an issue of Vie des Arts*)*

YVETTE: Always have to have the last word, don't you?

LUCILLE: Yes ... always.

YVETTE: Is it really that important?

LUCILLE: Absolutely. My dear sister, never give your opponent the advantage. You should always add something to what others say. It doesn't matter what, but something.

YVETTE: *(Looking at her)* Two to one for you!

LUCILLE: What I'm saying is not empty, Yvette, not at all. It's a lesson learned from our beloved Mother! In any case, there's no point in keeping score, today "Ch'us t'en forme" and I'm gonna win!

YVETTE: "Ch'us t'en forme." If Fernande heard you!

LUCILLE: If Fernande heard me, she would correct me and I would apologize, after having said, "Pardon, je suis z'en forme," with the liaison in the right place. I would assume an air of contrition and put on a face of shameful defeat ... and to myself, I'd tell her to go take a shit!

YVETTE: Lucille!

LUCILLE: It's in the dictionary, Yvette, and I pronounced it correctly.

(Silence)

LUCILLE: Do you remember the time ... oh, I was about six, I guess ... we went to look up that word in the dictionary ... Our two sisters were with us ... You said it couldn't be in the dictionary and Fernande said it was, but "in the pages for adults!"

YVETTE: I remember no such thing!

LUCILLE: You're right, it was "cock" we were looking for.

YVETTE: Honestly!

LUCILLE: Don't be a hypocrite! You remember perfectly well. It was one of those rainy afternoons when Mother'd play bridge with the great-grandniece of Sir Wilfrid Laurier, the great-granddaughter of Henri Bourassa, and the last gasp in the Louis Frechette clan; she, who had no luminaries in her obscure background and who always said: "In my family tree, the celebrities aren't in the past, but in the future! I prefer the young buds to the old branches!" Our mother was a run-of-the-mill Tremblay and so ashamed of it, she'd pretend to have a bone caught in her throat if someone asked where she came from ... Anyway ... You remember that day when the words "coitus," "clitoris" and "cock" made our afternoon, we, the four Beaugrand sisters, in organdy dresses and patent leather shoes? When we finally put the dictionary back, we'd been laughing so hard, all the pages of the letter "C" were a wreck. I even remember that when I said, "penis," you said: "That's what the priest makes you say at confession," and Fernande said: "No, it was penance, but whenever you say that word, you have to go to confession!"

YVETTE: And you said: "For my penis, I'll say five Our Fathers!" Only six years old!

LUCILLE: You see, you remember!

(YVETTE smiles a little and blushes a lot)

YVETTE: How did you know that word at that age?

LUCILLE: Lorraine was always saying it because Mother had forbidden it.

YVETTE: And you knew what it meant?

LUCILLE: No, but I knew it had something to do with men. I thought maybe it was a moustache!

YVETTE: *(Amused)* Really?

LUCILLE: Come on, Yvette: I knew perfectly well what it was. Mother was at least smart enough to tell us there were differences between little boys and girls, although the word "penis" would have made her heart skip, so she used something else.

(There is a short silence)

YVETTE: Even then, you liked to shock us.

LUCILLE: And if I still shock you, it's because you love it! There is no one less offensive than me.

(There is another short silence)

YVETTE: Poor Mother ... She'd have been much happier if she'd been able to lean on the family tree, even if she despised it, because frankly, the new shoots haven't borne much fruit ...

LUCILLE: Now, now. Don't despair. Who knows, there may yet be a great man lurking among the monsters born to our sister Fernande. Unless it's a sign of genius, eh, the congenital stutter of the latest bambino from the loins of the traitorous Lorraine ... I'll tell you this much, if there is a genius hiding in our family, he's very, very, very clever ... No, I'm sure Mother would have chosen to believe that one of her daughters had given birth to a brilliant dissembler.

YVETTE: All the same, this generation's growing up a bit too fast for my liking ... Do you realize that Nelligan, Fernande's youngest, is almost 20? It's terrible!

LUCILLE: Stop! You're making me dizzy! You don't mention rope in a hanged man's house!

YVETTE: My God, it's true! I haven't even wished you Happy Birthday!

LUCILLE: I know, you were waiting to sock me in the chops with it. I saw you coming.

(YVETTE gets up and goes to kiss her sister)

YVETTE: Happy Birthday, little pigeon. I know, 40 years hurts, but don't worry, it's only the beginning of your troubles!

LUCILLE: *(Laughing)* You see how you never manage to be truly nasty? The number of times you could have dropped that on me since this morning! When I told you at lunch, for instance, that your dress makes you look like a defrocked nun, all you had to say was "Happy Birthday" and you'd have scored five points.

YVETTE: I try to avoid the facile.

(They kiss each other again, very tenderly)

Let's call a truce for today ... It's a special day ...

LUCILLE: Capitulate at 40! Never! Be it for one single day! Go on, hide behind your Vie des Arts and I'll make you blush until Fernande arrives with her tiny gateau and Lorraine shows up with her cake the size of a barn.

(YVETTE blushes, ill at ease)

Yes, Yvette, I know the little tea you've organized for this afternoon is a birthday party ... I'm not a complete imbecile ... At least, not yet ... The four illustrious Beaugrand sisters will meet again in mutual massacre, according to tradition.

YVETTE: The massacre is not necessary, you know! It's you and Fernande who always start ... you like fighting so much ...

LUCILLE: You love it too, like everyone else! Admit it, a little impromptu without incident would bore you to tears! Whereas a rip-roaring battle with cake flying across the living-room, a little weeping and much gnashing of teeth, now, that is worthy of us! Remember the fun we had last year? We almost came to blows!

YVETTE: I was so embarrassed ... on my birthday ...

LUCILLE: What a souvenir! ... Lorraine's cake was so ugly and Fernande's so chic, you'd have thought they came from two different planets.

YVETTE: I bought you a real present, you know, but I won't give it to you 'til tea ... In front of everyone. Right after the cake ...

LUCILLE: But I don't have to FINISH the cake to collect my present ...

YVETTE: Stop it ...

LUCILLE: Imagine, slogging through Lorraine's mountain of pink and green icing, studded with silver pearls that stick in your teeth ...

YVETTE: Yech ... Lucille ...

LUCILLE: Not to mention the rock-hard sugar roses that taste of dust after three months in the window.

YVETTE: Lucille, stop!

LUCILLE: And how about the cake itself? Soggy cardboard!

(YVETTE fans herself with her Vie des Arts)

And all the while, Fernande's midget cream-puff waits in vain in the center of the table ... Did you ever notice, Yvette, that even though we laugh at Lorraine's cakes, we always dive into them first?

YVETTE: It's to make her happy ...

LUCILLE: Wrong! It's to make us happy! So we can have a good laugh after! And it gives you and me something to talk about, once they've gone and we're alone again ...

YVETTE: Oh, that's nice, tell me I'm ennuyante!

LUCILLE: Ennuyeuse, Yvette, ennuyeuse ... If Fernande heard you!
(Speaking affectionately)
Yes, Yvette, I do find you ennuyante! You and your "Remember Me" make a perfect couple!

YVETTE: You, on the other hand, are not all ... ennuyante!

LUCILLE: Certainly not. If it weren't for me, ennui would stalk this house, year in, year out. It would even choose the records! The same ones!

YVETTE: You just keep it up and you won't get your present.

LUCILLE: Yvette! Blackmail at your age! Shame on you! Besides, I already know what it is.

YVETTE: What do you mean, you know?

LUCILLE: Yvette, you always hide your presents in the same place! I've known for at least 10 years where you put them and I ALWAYS know at least a month in advance what it is you've bought me for Christmas or for my birthday.

YVETTE: And you never told me?

LUCILLE: I can't help it, I'm curious. And I prefer to know ahead of time ... to hide my disappointment and work up an expression of joy and satisfaction.
(YVETTE stands. She is on the verge of tears)
Come on, Yvette, you know I'm only teasing ... If you're still going to use blackmail at 46, you can at least let me be a tease at 40! Good Lord ...
(She goes over to her sister)
Yvette, I think you are an absolutely fascinating person and it would never enter my mind that you're a bore ... You happy now?

YVETTE: You're still making fun of me!

LUCILLE: I have always pulled your leg, but you keep sticking it out! It's almost too easy now. If you're not careful, I'm going to look for another partner!

YVETTE: I know you're teasing, but at times you go too far ...

LUCILLE: I try to avoid the facile, too, you know ...

YVETTE: Well, believe me, you've succeeded!

LUCILLE: *(Smiling)* Thank you! Now, sit back down and blow your nose, our sisters will think I've made a martyr of you again!

YVETTE: They'd almost be right.

LUCILLE: Yes ... almost. Alas!
(YVETTE has sat down again. LUCILLE puts her Vie des Arts on her lap)
I have no idea where you hide your presents, nor that you bought me a Cuisinart for my birthday. And I didn't try it out the other day when you went shopping for gloves at Ogilvy's ...
(YVETTE has started, but she doesn't answer)
I'll go heat up your tea ...

INDIAN

George Ryga

Place: "flat, grey, stark non-country"
Time: unspecified; the play was published in 1971
Characters: Indian, Watson

"Indian" is an indictment of white attitudes toward North American
 Indians. The boss Watson is a cruel man; he locks Indian's son in a
 granary and threatens to shoot the boy if Indian disappears before
 his work (building a fence) is done.

The following scene is from the beginning of the play. At curtain rise,
 Indian is asleep, hat over his face, on the ground. Watson discovers
 him.

*Curtain up on INDIAN asleep, using slight hump of earth under his neck for
 pillow. He is facing sun, with hat over his face. WATSON approaches from
 stage right, dragging his feet and raising dust. Stops over INDIAN's head.*
WATSON: *(Loud and angry)* Hey! What the hell! Come on ... you aimin'
 to die like that?
 *(INDIAN clutches his hat and sits up. Lifts his hat and looks up, then jerks
 hat down over his face)*
INDIAN: Oy! Oooh! The sun she blind me, goddamn! ... Boss ... I am
 sick! Head, she gonna explode, sure as hell!
 *(He tries to lie down again, but WATSON grabs his arm and yanks him to
 his feet)*
WATSON: There's gonna be some bigger explosions if I don't get
 action out of you guys. What happened now? Where's the fat boy?
 An' the guy with the wooden leg?
INDIAN: Jus' a minute, boss. Don't shout like that. *(Looks carefully
 around him)* They not here ... Guess they run away, boss - no? ... Roy,
 he's not got wooden leg. He got bone leg same's you an' me. Only
 it dried up and look like wood. Small, too ... *(Lifts up his own right leg)*
 That shoe ... that was fit Roy's bad leg. The other shoe is tight. But
 this one, boss - she is hunder times tighter!
WATSON: *(Squatting)* Is them Limpy's boots?
INDIAN: Sure, boss. I win them at poker las' night. Boss, what a time
 we have - everybody go haywire!

(WATSON looks around impatiently.)

WATSON: I can see. Where's your tent?

INDIAN: *(Pointing to ashes)* There she is. Sonofabitch, but I never see anything burn like that before!

WATSON: The kid wasn't lying. You guys DID burn the tent.

INDIAN: What kid?

WATSON: Your kid.

INDIAN: *(Jumping to his feet)* Alphonse? Where is Alphonse? He run away when Sam and Roy start fight ...

WATSON: Yeh, he run away ... run all the way to the house. Told us you guys was drunk an' wild. So the missus fixed him something to eat and put him to bed.

INDIAN: He's all right? Oh, that's good, boss!

WATSON: *(Smiling grimly)* Sure, he's all right. Like I said, the missus fed the kid. Then I took him and put him in the granary, lockin' the door so he ain't gonna get out. That's for protection.

INDIAN: Protection? You don't need protection, boss. Alphonse not gonna hurt you.

WATSON: Ha! Ha! Ha! Big joke! ... Where are your pals as was gonna help you with this job? Where are they - huh?

INDIAN: I don't know. They run away when tent catch fire.

WATSON: Great! That's just great! You know what you guys done to me? Yesterday, ya nicked me for 10 dollars ... I'm hungry, the fat boy says to me - my stomach roar like thunder. He's gonna roar out the other end before I'm finished with you an' him! How much you figure the fence you put up is worth?

INDIAN: *(Rubbing his eyes and trying to see the fence in the distance)* I dunno, boss. You say job is worth 40 dollars. Five, mebbe 10 dollars done ...

WATSON: Five dollars! Look here, smart guy - ya've got 29 posts in - I counted 'em. At 10 cents apiece, you've done two dollars 90 cents worth of work! An' you got 10 dollars off me yesterday!

INDIAN: *(Pondering sadly)* Looks like you in the hole, boss.

WATSON: Well, maybe I am ... an' maybe I ain't. I got your kid in the granary locked up so he'll keep. You try to run off after your pals, an' I'm gonna take my gun an' shoot a hole that big through the kid's head!

(He makes a ring with his fingers to show exact size of injury he intends to make)

INDIAN: No!

WATSON: Oh, sure! So what ya say, Indian? ... You gonna work real hard and be a good boy?

INDIAN: Boss - you know me. I work! Them other guys is no good - but not Johnny I make deal - I keep deal! You see yourself I stay when they run.

WATSON: Sure, ya stayed. You were too goddamned drunk to move, that's why you stayed! What goes on in your heads ... ah, hell! You ain't worth the bother!

INDIAN: No, no, boss ... You all wrong.

WATSON: Get to work! It's half past nine, and you ain't even begun to think about the fence.

INDIAN: Boss ... a little bit later. I sick man ... head - she hurt to burst. An' stomach - ugh! Boss, I not eat anything since piece of baloney yesterday ...

WATSON: *(Turning angrily)* You go to hell- you hear me? Go to hell! I got that story yesterday. Now g'wan - I wanna see some action!

INDIAN: Alright, boss. You know me. You trust me.

WATSON: Trust ya! I wouldn't trust you with the time of day, goddamn you! *(Remembers something)* Hey - there's a snoop from the Indian Affairs department toolin' around today - checkin' on all you guys workin' off the reserve. I'm telling you somethin' ... you're working for me, so if you got any complaints, you better tell me now. I don't want no belly-achin' to no government guys.

INDIAN: Complaints? ... Me? I happy, boss. What you take me for?

WATSON: Sure, sure ... Now get back to work. An' remember what I told you ... you try to beat it, an' I shoot the kid. You understand? *(INDIAN removes his hat and wipes his brow)*

INDIAN: Sure, bossman - I understand.

(INDIAN looks towards the fence in the fields. WATSON stands behind him, scratching his chin and smirking insolently. INDIAN glances back at him, then shrugging with resignation, moves unsteadily to the unfinished fence post. He pulls the box nearer to the post, picks up hammer and is about to step on the box. Changes his mind and sits for a moment on the box, hammer across his knees. Rubs his eyes and forehead)

WATSON: Now what the hell's the matter? Run out of gas?

INDIAN: Oh, boss ... If I be machine that need only gas, I be all right mebbe ...

WATSON: So you going to sit an' let the day go by? ... Indian, I've got lots of time, and I can grind you to dirt if you're figurin' on bustin' my ass!

INDIAN: Nobody bust you, boss. I be all right right away ... Sementos! But the head she is big today. An' stomach ... she is slop-bucket full of turpentine. Boss ... two dollars a quart, Sam Cardinal says to me ... with four dollars we get enough bad whiskey to poison every Indian from here to Lac La Biche! Sam Cardinal tell the truth that time for sure ...

WATSON: What kind of rubbish did you drink?

INDIAN: Indian whiskey, boss. You know what is Indian whiskey?

WATSON: No. You tell me, an' then you get to work!

INDIAN: Sure, boss, sure. As soon as field stop to shake. Indian whiskey

... you buy two quart. You get one quart wood alcohol ... maybe half quart formalin, an' the rest is water from sick horse! That's the kind whiskey they make for Indian.

WATSON: An' it makes the field shake for you ... Christ! YOU make me sick!!

INDIAN: Oh, but what party it make!

WATSON: *(Irritably)* Come on ... come on! Get on with it.

(INDIAN scrambles on box and starts to drive post into ground. He stops after a few seconds. He is winded)

INDIAN: Sementos! Is hard work, boss! ... I tell you, Sam Cardinal sing like sick cow ... an' Roy McIntosh dance on his bad leg. Funny! ... Alphonse an' I laugh until stomach ache. I win Roy's boots in poker, but he dance anyhow. Then Sam get mad an' he push Roy ... Roy push him back ... They fight ... Boy, I hungry now, boss ...

WATSON: Tough! I wanna see 10 bucks of work done.

INDIAN: Then you feed me? Big plate potatoes an' meat? ... An' mebbe big hunk of pie?

WATSON: *(Laughs sarcastically)* Feed ya? Soon's I get my 10 bucks squared away, you can lie down and die! But not on my field ... go on the road allowance!

(INDIAN hits the post a few more times, trying to summon up strength to get on with the work. But it is all in vain. Drops hammer heavily to the box. Rubs his stomach)

INDIAN: You hard man, boss ... hard like iron. Sam is bad man ... bugger up you, bugger up me. Get 10 dollars for grub from you ... almost like steal 10 dollars from honest man. Buy whiskey ... buy baloney an' two watermelon. He already eat most of baloney and I see him give hunk to friendly dog. I kick dog. Sam get mad ... why you do that? Dog is nothing to you? I say, he eat my grub. He can go catch cat if he hungry. I catch an' eat cat once myself, boss ... winter 1956. Not much meat an' tough like rope. I never eat cat again, that's for sure. Sementos! But the head hurt!

WATSON: One more word, Indian ... just one more word an' I'm gonna clean house on you! ... You wanna try me? Come on!

(For a moment the INDIAN teeters between two worlds, then with a violent motion he sweeps up the hammer and begins pounding the post, mechanically with incredible rhythm of defeat. WATSON watches for a while, his anger gone now. Scratches himself nervously, then makes a rapid exit off stage left)

(Almost immediately the hammering begins to slow, ending with one stroke when the hammer head rests on the post, and INDIAN's head droops on his outstretched arms)

INDIAN: Scared talk ... world is full of scared talk. I show scare an' I get a job from Mister Watson. Scared Indian is a live Indian. My head don't get Alphonse free ... but hands do.

THE LAST BUS
Raymond Storey

Place: Eileen's kitchen, a small town
Time: early Saturday morning; year unspecified; the play was first
produced in 1987
Characters: Robert, his brother Gary

Having taken a leave of absence from his job as music teacher in a
private school, Robert has come back to his hometown, ostensibly to
attend the funeral of his best friend Marty but also to avoid a nervous
breakdown. The homecoming forces Robert to come to terms with
his past, and especially with his homosexual love for Marty—a love
not likely to be tolerated in this small town, a love that was neither
entirely understood nor reciprocated by Marty. Through it all,
Robert's homosexuality has remained a secret shared only with
Marty.

Robert comes home the night before Marty's funeral. In the scene
below, he and his older brother Gary reflect upon Marty's death and
upon the vicissitudes of life in a small town. Gary is a video arcade
freak whose future seems fairly bleak and directionless. As the scene
begins, he is spooning cereal into his mouth and watching Star Trek
on television. He drinks the milk from his cereal bowl as Robert
enters.

*GARY enters and turns on the TV. Saturday morning. Captain Kirk is engaged
in black and white combat. GARY watches Star Trek as he spoons the last
of his cereal into his mouth. As he drinks the remaining milk from the bowl,
ROBERT enters.*
GARY: 'Morning, Rob.
ROBERT: Good morning.
GARY: You want some Shreddies?
ROBERT: No thanks. *(ROBERT lowers the volume on the TV)* Do you
mind?
GARY: No, that's okay. I seen it. What time you get in?
ROBERT: Around one, I guess.
GARY: Did you see Mom?
ROBERT: No. She was asleep. What time is it?

GARY: 11:30. Day's half over. Where'd you go? The hotel?

ROBERT: Yeah.

GARY: What I thought. Mom stopped by the funeral home. Guess you didn't go, huh. You want some coffee?

ROBERT: What kind of coffee?

GARY: Coffee coffee.

ROBERT: Instant?

GARY: Yeah.

ROBERT: I guess so.

(GARY gets up and plugs in the kettle)

GARY: Anybody in there last night?

ROBERT: It was packed. I spoke to Kelly Wilks a bit. He was sitting over on the Escorts side with a bunch. I just had a couple of beers in the Gents Only. They were pretty tanked up. I didn't feel like seeing any of them.

GARY: The hotel's real changed, eh?

ROBERT: I didn't notice much.

GARY: Well, the Escorts side more than the Gents Only. They torn the bandstand out, and made the dance floor bigger. They got a deejay there on the weekends. And they took out the pool table and put in some other games - Pac Man and Space Commander. You ever play Space Commander?

ROBERT: No.

GARY: Oh, it's a real neat one. You have this guy with a gun, right - you only get three plays for a quarter - and you can only go this way - back and forth. Okay? So, all of a sudden, these big purple things - space ships sorta - come down from the sky and start shooting at you with their lasers. Now, you can only dodge this way, right? But they can fly anywheres and boy, do they ever. Up, down, in, out, back and forth and you have to try not to be hit by a laser and stay the hell out of the way at the same time. But what you really want to do is work it so that you can get right underneath one of them buggers, 'cuz then you can blast the shit out of them. After you blasted all of them purples, these other things start coming at you, and they are really moving. They're green and they kinda look like pigs, except they got wings, and they're dive-bombing you, right? Like, trying to blast you, right? So you gotta blast all of them first. And then, this big, holy mother of a thing comes barrelling straight for you. It's sorta like a flying steamroller, eh ...

ROBERT: So, wait a minute. What are you winning here?

GARY: Oh, you don't win nothing. You don't win nothing in any of these games.

ROBERT: So, what's the point?

GARY: To see how many of them buggers you can blast before they get you. You know. Just ... you just keep going and keep blasting them for as long as you can. Get over 200,000 and you get to be High Commander. But ... nobody done that yet. You don't win nothing. You wanna go over and try it? You get three plays for a quarter. It's something to do.

ROBERT: I suppose it is. Gary, how's the job hunting going?

(GARY notices that the kettle is boiling. He makes the instant)

GARY: Oh, no. Hotel don't open 'til noon. What do you take? Double double?

ROBERT: Black. You got any prospects?

GARY: Funeral's at 1:30. We could try the hotel after.

ROBERT: Gary?

GARY: I had a interview about a week ago or so. They were looking for a warehouse manager at the Co-op. It looked real good there for a while, but they said that I didn't have enough job-related experience. They said they coulda maybe give me a job as stock boy, eh - but shit, they wanted me to take it at minimum wage. So, I told them to shove it up their you-knows. It wouldn't be worth my while. To go off the pogey? I was earning nearly twice that at Purvis's before they closed up shop. There's nothing around here. I look in the paper every day, but there's nothing. The only job they advertised all last week was dew worm picking. Can you believe that? Picking fucking dew worms for a living? I didn't know white people was allowed to do that kinda work. *(GARY sets the mug of coffee in front of ROBERT)* So, little bro, you like teaching at this private school?

ROBERT: It's a job.

GARY: Them rich kids give you a lot of airs and so on?

ROBERT: They're just kids. I don't think half of them even realize that they're well off. They think everybody has three meals a day, a four-car garage and a Betamax in the bedroom.

GARY: I wish. The buggers.

ROBERT: It's not their fault. Things are handed to them. They just take them. There's one kid. A boy in my junior class. Reminds me of Marty. Looks like him a bit, and he can play anything he picks up. But he doesn't have the burn ... He couldn't care less. And no matter what else you've got going for you, if you don't have the burn, you still have nothing. Burn. What am I talking about? He's better off without it. He doesn't know how lucky he is. *(ROBERT sips his coffee)* Aw, jumpin! Gary. This is awful coffee.

GARY: I don't know how it could be. All you do is put in the water.

ROBERT: You think Marty did it on purpose, don't you, Gary?

GARY: I don't know. There was no skid marks to speak of. And he sure made a mess of them guard rails. It just looks like he gunned her and went for it.

ROBERT: He wouldn't do that, Gary.

GARY: It don't make much sense. He had a good job. I know that ain't everything but he coulda hung on at the foundry until retirement, and that's something that a lot of people can't say.

ROBERT: I guess.

GARY: He got along with everybody, same as ever. And all that stuff that Mom was saying about Blair was a crock. I'll tell you. If getting a regular piece of tail is a reason to kill yourself, it's the first time I ever heard of it. There was some problems with his folks, I guess maybe ... I dunno. Him and Blair might've been having a bit of trouble - I heard something about that - but I guess Blair's the only one who knows anything for sure. And she's not talking to nobody. I dunno. Why do you think he done it?

ROBERT: Me? I couldn't tell you.

GARY: Well, people been asking me, eh. I mean, I think everyone sorta ... I don't know.

ROBERT: What?

GARY: I think everyone kinda expects that you will know something. I mean, you guys were always together.

ROBERT: When we were kids. A lot of things changed. Everybody thinks that nothing changes out there, because nothing changes around here. Things change. People change. God, I know I have.

GARY: Things change here, too.

ROBERT: Sure, a new coat of paint on the old bandhall. A new dance floor in the hotel. Johnson's house may have burned down on Elgin Street, but it's still the same street.

GARY: Not to the Johnsons. You don't think Marty changed?

ROBERT: *(Pause)* No. No, he probably didn't. Too smart in too many things. Too dumb in others.

GARY: Oh sure. Dumb like a fox.

ROBERT: Maybe, Gary.

GARY: I was just curious, because ... well, I was just wondering if there was something specific that he mighta told you.

ROBERT: Like when?

GARY: Last Christmas. When you was home. You was bugged about something. That time he gave you his guitar.

ROBERT: That was different. It was Christmas. He didn't play it anymore.

(GARY shrugs)

GARY: 'Member you guys playing over at the hotel. Your duo. The Lords of Light.

ROBERT: What a joke.

GARY: No way. Everybody said it. Come on, they used to buy me beers, and you were just my kid brother. Everybody said you shoulda gone for it.

ROBERT: We weren't good enough.

GARY: Wouldn't that have been something? The two of you ... like, on talk shows or something.

ROBERT: We weren't good enough.

GARY: Well, I dunno ...

ROBERT: Yeah, well I do!

GARY: Hey, whatever you say buddy.

ROBERT: *(Getting up)* Where is Mom?

GARY: She's gone over to Ruth Grant's. They got a bunch over there making sandwiches for after the funeral. Supposedly. Angie Grant is marrying Dave Crawford next Saturday, I figure this the old birds' excuse to get over and have a good gawk at Angie and Dave's loot - keeping a running tally on the tea towels and toasters. She should be home soon.

ROBERT: I don't want to go to the funeral, Gary.

GARY: How come?

ROBERT: I've got lots to remember Marty by. I don't need to paw through it with the rest of the town.

GARY: So what do you feel like doing?

ROBERT: I dunno. Go for a walk.

GARY: Wanna go over and visit Tim Bursey?

ROBERT: At the hotel? And do what?

GARY: Blast some of them green things, buddy. Them pigs with wings. Three plays for a quarter. Come on, let's go visit ol' Tim.

ROBERT: Why not.

GARY: Sit tight. I'm gonna go check my quarter situation.

(GARY exits. ROBERT takes a last gulp of his coffee and grimaces)

THE LAST BUS

Raymond Storey

Place: Eileen's kitchen
Time: late Saturday night
Characters: Eileen, her son Robert

Robert attends Marty's funeral and, later that day, visits Marty's ex-girlfriend Blair. She tells Robert how Marty crashed his car and died. Apparently, the gossip around town is that Marty's death was a suicide.

The following scene takes place in Eileen's house, late the same night, as Robert returns from his visit with Blair.

In the kitchen. The TV is off the air, and static fills the screen. It is late. ROBERT moves into the darkened kitchen. He picks up a guitar and cradles it. EILEEN enters.

EILEEN: Robbie? I thought that was you.

ROBERT: Yeah, it's me. I thought you'd be asleep.

EILEEN: No. I was just lying there looking at the light fixture. What are you doing sitting in the dark?

ROBERT: Do you have to be up early?

EILEEN: No, no. I'm on afternoons all this week. I can stay in bed just like a lady of leisure. Just make sure I drag this old carcass outta there by two.

ROBERT: That's a deal.

(EILEEN snaps on the light)

EILEEN: It's real bad for you to sit in the dark. *(Sitting down)* Would you look at this old table. Ain't it a mess, though? Kinda funny how you can have something around for years and years and never really look at it. My gol, it's ugly. I ordered this thing outta the catalogue. It was the cheapest set in the book - we always had to get the cheapest - but it looked real good in the picture. They always do, don't they. Of course, when it come I hated it.

ROBERT: Why did you keep it then?

EILEEN: Oh, I don't know. It was here. And it was a darned sight better than what we had. Someday I'll throw it out and buy me a new one. After I won the lottery maybe. Boys oh boys, but there's a heckuva lot I'd do if I ever won that lottery.

ROBERT: Now, Mother. Don't tell me you're looking for money to buy you happiness.

EILEEN: Well, they say it don't, I guess. But I am telling you, it would make misery a darned sight more interesting.

ROBERT: Maybe.

EILEEN: You was over visiting Blair Dean, eh?

ROBERT: Yeah. For a while. She's pretty disoriented, the poor kid.

EILEEN: Well, she's pitiful, all right.

ROBERT: Come on, Ma.

EILEEN: I didn't say nothing. You was there for quite a while. Did you have a nice visit?

ROBERT: I don't know if that's how I'd describe it.

EILEEN: What'd you talk about?

ROBERT: Not much. It's funny, you know, we don't really know each other, really. She didn't have any food in the house, so I took her over to the China Valley for a bite to eat.

EILEEN: Hmm. No food in the house.

ROBERT: She needs somebody around, Mom. Don't pick on her. It must have been the same for you when you lost Dad.

EILEEN: Well, hardly is it the same! When your father died, we was married 17 years. After 17 years of marriage, you can practically hear a man thinking - you're like one person! They sure was nothing like one person! She didn't even know that boy wanted to kill hisself. Hardly is that the same. Robbie, you may think I'm a fool, but I ain't. You don't just get two weeks off in the middle of the year.

ROBERT: What's that?

EILEEN: They wouldn't just give you two weeks off in the middle of the year for nothing.

ROBERT: No. They wouldn't.

EILEEN: You didn't quit did you?

ROBERT: No, I didn't quit.

EILEEN: 'Cuz if you quit your job, you're gonna be real sorry. Teaching jobs is no easier to find than any other. Bernice and Edgar Bursey's girl Carol went through for a teacher and she still hasn't found a job ...

ROBERT: I just took some time off. Sick time. I'm entitled to it.

EILEEN: You're not sick.

ROBERT: I'm not going to die. I just need some time off. A couple of weeks. I just need some time to pull things back together. I don't know, Mom. I feel like it's slipping away from me.

EILEEN: What is?

ROBERT: I thought, for a while, that I could get something from teaching that I needed. You know? I thought it could get me by. But it doesn't. It doesn't because I shouldn't be there for me, I should be there for them. And I'm not. It doesn't because I don't belong in a classroom. And I don't know where I do belong.

EILEEN: You're a good teacher, Robbie. I know that.

ROBERT: It's that kind of panic, you know. Like when Marty and I used to race across the river. It feels like that. Like when we'd be out in the middle somewhere, and I'm scared, you know - my heart's pounding, because we're too far out and I'm scared I can't reach either bank. And there's nothing to hang on to ... But at least then ... Never mind. It doesn't matter.

EILEEN: I know how you mean.

ROBERT: I'm just tired, Mom. Don't listen to me, okay?

EILEEN: You know, most of the time you're only as alone as you want to be.

ROBERT: Yeah, right.

EILEEN: I wish I could think of something to say that would make you feel better about it, but I can't think of nothing. Just don't lose that job, Robbie. Was you playing something, Rob? I haven't heard you play nothing in so long. Why don't you play me something?

ROBERT: No. It's too late, Ma. I'm too tired.

EILEEN: Well, go to bed then.

ROBERT: I just want to sit here for a while, okay?

EILEEN: *(Getting up from the table)* You'll see that these lights get out, eh?

ROBERT: Yep.

EILEEN: Don't sit up too long, Robbie.

ROBERT: 'Night.

> *(EILEEN exits. ROBERT holds the guitar to him.)*

THE MELVILLE BOYS

Norm Foster

Place: at a lake, a cabin belonging to Lee's uncle
Time: the present, evening, mid-September
Characters: Lee Melville, mid-30s; Mary, early 30s

Lee Melville is dying of cancer; he has a year to live. He and his younger
brother Owen arrive at their uncle's cabin, where they plan to spend
some quality time together. There they meet two sisters Mary and
Loretta and, at Owen's insistence, escort them to a dance at the local
Legion Hall.

After the dance, all four of them return to the cabin. Owen, who is
engaged to be married, grabs some cans of beer and heads out to the
lake for a skinny dip with Loretta. Lee, who is married, remains in the
cabin with Mary—it's a safer place to be, especially since Mary has
been characterized, by her sister, as "the original nice girl."

LEE: *(Moving left, to the door)* Owen? Owen! *(To MARY)* He shouldn't be
doing that, you know. He's getting married in less than a month.
(Yelling) Owen? *(To MARY)* I thought your sister didn't like the water.
MARY: *(Moving right)* Oh, she doesn't mind swimming in it. It's riding
on top of it she doesn't like. *(Sits on the couch)*
LEE: Well, does she know she's out there with an engaged man?
MARY: Oh, I don't think it would matter if she did.
LEE: You mean, she doesn't care? *(Picks up the beer that Owen dropped,
and puts it back in the fridge)*
MARY: Well, actually, Loretta only really cares about Loretta. I've
always envied her for that.
LEE: Envied her? For being selfish?
MARY: Sure. It's easier to make decisions that way. You just decide to
do what's best for you, and you don't worry about how it affects
anybody else. Don't you think it would be easier that way?
LEE: *(Moving to look out the screen door again)* I wouldn't know.
MARY: Of course you wouldn't. You've never tried it.

LEE: *(Moving right, towards MARY)* What makes you say that?

MARY: Oh, I can tell.

LEE: How?

MARY: Well, for instance, you didn't want to go to the dance tonight, but you went because your brother wanted to go. I got the feeling you didn't want us around this morning, but you didn't kick us out. And you probably don't want us here right now, but you haven't asked us to leave.

LEE: Is that right? Well, I'll have you know I can be pretty selfish when I want to be.

MARY: No, I don't think so.

LEE: *(Moving right and sitting beside MARY)* Oh, yes I can. As a matter of fact, I did something tonight that was selfish. Something that was in my best interests.

MARY: And what was that?

LEE: I didn't eat any of your cake.
(MARY and LEE both laugh)

MARY: You're right. That was selfish.
(An awkward pause. LEE gets up and moves back to the screen door left) Anyway, it looks like we're stuck here for a while. At least until those two cool off. *(Gets up and moves to LEE)* So, what do you want to do?

LEE: *(Nervously)* Do?

MARY: Yeah. You want to do something?

LEE: Listen, I should tell you that I'm a married man.

MARY: *(Slightly offended)* Well, I guess that rules out getting married then, doesn't it? You want to play cards? *(Moves upstage behind the table)*

LEE: I'm sorry. I don't know why I said that.

MARY: *(Getting a fork from the cupboard upstage center)* It was a very innocent question.

LEE: I know. I guess I was just protecting myself.

MARY: From what? From me? The original nice girl? *(Picks up one of the plates off the counter and sets it on the table)*

LEE: I don't know. Maybe.

MARY: Well, listen, I'm married too.

LEE: *(Relieved)* Oh. I didn't know that.

MARY: You didn't ask. *(Moves upstage, to the fridge)*

LEE: So, where's your husband tonight?

MARY: I'm not sure. *(Opens the fridge and takes out a beer)*

LEE: Well, is he out of town?

MARY: Oh, he's out of town all right. *(Holding up the beer)* Do you mind?

LEE: No, go ahead.

MARY: You see, technically I'm still married. He left me two years ago. *(Moves to the table and sits; cuts herself a piece of cake and puts it on the plate)*

LEE: Oh, I'm sorry.

MARY: Yeah, me too.

LEE: Why did he leave? *(Sits at the table)*

MARY: I don't know. He didn't tell me.

LEE: He didn't tell you why?

MARY: He didn't tell me he was leaving. I woke up one morning and he was gone. He left me a note saying he'd send some money for the car.

LEE: He took the car too?

MARY: *(Affirmative)* Hm-hmm. Oh, I don't blame him for that. I mean, if I was going to leave, I'd take the car.
(MARY takes a bit of the cake, and then tries to hide the fact that it tastes awful. LEE, smiling, opens her beer for her and places it in front of her. She takes a drink)

LEE: So, do you have any idea where he is?

MARY: Who?

LEE: Your husband.

MARY: Oh. Uh, well, he's probably down south somewhere. He always said he wanted to move south. I would've moved with him, but he never asked.

LEE: Well, if you don't mind my saying so, this guy sounds like a jerk.

MARY: Yeah, I thought so too, at the time.

LEE: And what about now?

MARY: Now? Now, I wish he'd come back.

LEE: Come back? You wouldn't take him back?

MARY: Sure. Why not?

LEE: After all this time? After the way he left?

MARY: I miss him. I guess I still love him.

LEE: The man took your car! He didn't tell you he was leaving. He didn't even have the decency to tell you why!

MARY: I think he felt trapped.

LEE: Oh, come on. That's the oldest excuse in the world. Everybody feels trapped. Don't you think I feel trapped once in a while?

MARY: How should I know? I met you this morning.

LEE: Well, I do. A lot of the time!

MARY: So, why don't you leave?

LEE: We're not talking about me. We're talking about your husband. *(Stands, and starts to pace)* I can't believe you'd take him back. Is this what you've been doing for the past two years? Sitting around waiting for this clown to come home with your car? God, that's such a waste!

MARY: You know, you're taking this harder than I did.

LEE: He's probably sold the car. You realize that. I mean, as far as he's concerned, it's party time. And that's what you should be thinking too. You should forget him. Find somebody else. Start dating.

MARY: Who says I haven't been dating?

LEE: Not if you're still waiting for him, you haven't been.

MARY: Well, what about tonight?

LEE: What about tonight?

MARY: Isn't this a date?

LEE: *(Getting nervous again)* What ... this? You mean, you and me? No, this is not a date.

MARY: Well, what is it then?

LEE: Uh ... well ... it's more like a car pool.

MARY: A car pool?!! *(Gets up and storms to the couch)*

LEE: Well, no, not a car pool. It's more like ... like you and I are chaperoning Owen and Loretta. *(Moves to the screen door left and yells out)* Hey, are you two behaving yourselves out there?!

MARY: *(Putting on her lifejacket)* All right, don't worry about it. It's not a date. I'm too old for this silly dating business anyway.

LEE: *(Moving right)* Too old? No, you're not. No. You should get out there. Meet somebody. Somebody who appreciates you.

MARY: I already had somebody who appreciated me. At least, I thought he did. And look what happened.

LEE: So, find somebody else.

MARY: What, and make the same mistake again? No thank you.

LEE: Look, all I'm saying is, it's a waste. A waste of a terrific person. You shouldn't be alone.

MARY: I can get by alone.

LEE: Oh, sure you can get by. Anybody can GET BY, if that's all you want to do is GET BY! Is that all you want to do? Is that how you want to be remembered? As the girl who got by?! 'What kind of a girl was MARY, anyway? Oh, she got by. Was she a smart girl? Well, she got by. How was she at sex? Oh, she got by.'

MARY: I think I'd better go.

(MARY starts to move left but LEE stops her with his next speech)

LEE: You know what's worse than your husband leaving you? It's you, sitting around waiting for him to come back. Yeah, I'll tell you this. After I'm gone, Arlene's not going to sit around for long. No sir. She'll start dating, and in a few years she'll be married again. And she's older than you are, I'll bet. How old are you?

MARY: 31.

LEE: There you go. Arlene's 33.

MARY: What are you saying? Are you telling me you ARE leaving?

LEE: *(Moving back to the table)* No, I'm not leaving. I'm dying. And I don't want that to ruin Arlene's life. Look, you said you wanted to be a little more selfish. Well, now's a good time to start. Start doing what's best for you. *(Sits at the table)*

MARY: *(After a pause)* Can we back up here for just a second. Did you say 'I'm dying'?

LEE: *(Trying to cover it up now)* Uh ... I don't know. Maybe I did.

MARY: Yeah, well, I think you did. I'm pretty sure I heard 'I'm dying' in there somewhere.

LEE: All right, I said it. Let's just forget it, okay? Sometimes I get stuck for something to say, so I just blurt anything out.

MARY: You get stuck for something to say, so you say 'I'm dying'? I mean, I thought the conversation was going along fine. You were more than holding up your end. Didn't you think it was going along fine?

LEE: Yes, I did ....

MARY: Well, then, what the hell's 'I'm dying' supposed to mean?

LEE: I don't know why I said it. Maybe you seemed like the kind of person I could say it to without getting emotional.

MARY: Without who getting emotional?

LEE: You! ... and me. Both of us. I'd just like to talk about it once without somebody crying. I talk to my mother about it, and she cries. I talk to Arlene about it ... she cries. And Owen, well, he won't talk about it at all. I mean, I figured, you're not involved ... you hardly know me. What's to cry about? Right? I'm sorry. I shouldn't have brought it up. We won't talk about it anymore, okay?

MARY: *(Quietly)* Okay.

LEE: Okay.

MARY: *(After a short pause, trying to hold back the tears)* You really are dying, aren't you?

LEE: No.

MARY: Yes you are.

LEE: No, I'm not. I lied.

MARY: No, you are. You really are. *(Puts her hand over her mouth to stifle her next line)* Oh, my God. *(Turns away from LEE and takes a Kleenex out of the box on the shelf, left)*

LEE: What are you doing?

MARY: Nothing. *(On the verge of breaking down)*

LEE: What have you got there?

MARY: Nothing.

LEE: Is that a Kleenex? *(Stands up)*

MARY: No. *(Moves upstage to the stove, her back still turned to LEE)*

LEE: It is. It's Kleenex. What's it for?

MARY: It's for nothing.

LEE: No, it's for something. You don't just pick up a Kleenex for nothing.

MARY: Yes, you do.

LEE: No, you don't. Now, what's it for? Are you getting emotional?

MARY: No.

LEE: You are, aren't you? You're crying.

MARY: *(Turns to him in a tearful outburst)* I am not!!

LEE: *(Turning away)* Oh, God, not another one.

MARY: Well, I can't help it. I'm an emotional person.

LEE: But, we're practically strangers.

MARY: We've dated.

LEE: We haven't dated! This is not a date!!

MARY: *(Sitting at the table)* It doesn't matter. I'm an easy crier.

LEE: So, why didn't you tell me?

MARY: You didn't give me a chance! You just said 'I'm dying' out of nowhere. I didn't see it coming. You should've built up to it.

LEE: Built up to it?

MARY: Yes. Tell me you're not feeling well, and work up from there. *(Starts to eat the cake, in her despair)*

LEE: All right, I'm sorry. I had no idea it would affect you like this.

MARY: *(Crying and eating)* Oh, it's not just you. It's everything. I mean, here you are ... you seem like a nice guy. You've got a wife. You've probably got kids.

LEE: Two girls.

MARY: *(Moaning through her mouthful of cake)* Oh, there you go, you've got a family. And what happens? You're dying. And then, here I am ... I'm a good person, right? Things seem to be going along fine. I'm happy. Then bingo! Just like that, my husband skips town ... What a life!

MEMOIR

John Murrell

Place: the terrace of Sarah Bernhardt's seaside estate in Belle-Ile-en-Mer,
France
Time: late afternoon, summer, 1922
Characters: Sarah, Pitou

Seventy-seven years old and with an artificial leg, Sarah Bernhardt sits
in the sun and reflects upon her past. With the help of her middle-
aged secretary George Pitou, she is attempting to compose a second
volume of her memoirs. When her memory fails, they resort to a
game Pitou hates and Sarah loves—improvisation.

SARAH: Yes - we shall IMPROVISE! It always helps. You - you, Pitou,
shall be - my mother. Nagging, scolding, whining - you do it so well.
PITOU: I'm not an actor, Madame.
SARAH: And I shall be able to remember EVERYTHING!
PITOU: Madame, I - I can't!
SARAH: *(Holding out her hands to him, a rehearsed gesture of supplication)*
Pitou?!
PITOU: *(Rapidly)* There is nothing in my contract that requires me to
impersonate Madame's relatives and acquaintances! I informed
Madame of that fact the first time she suggested this nonsense and
I feel obliged at the present time to remind Madame of the terms of
our -!
SARAH: PITOU! YOU WILL DO IT!
(Pause)
PITOU: How do we start?
SARAH: I am - 27 years old.
PITOU: *(He starts to remonstrate, thinks better of it)* Just as you say,
Madame.
SARAH: *(Improvising)* I am living in Paris, on the Left Bank. With my
lover Prince Henri de Ligne and our darling little baby, our little
Maurice. *(In a different voice)* Where is Maurice?
PITOU: He took your granddaughters and Dr. Marot to fish for shrimp.
SARAH: Excellent, we won't be interrupted. Yes, the sun - never mind!
I am 27 years old. *(To him)* You are my beautiful mother -
PITOU: Madame, please -!

SARAH: *(Firmly)* You are my beautiful mother! You've come to nag and whine and perform the rest of your repertoire as you do regularly, every month! You are one of the most glamorous women in Paris, in France, which is to say, in the world. You have achieved affluence, Maman, and even - respectability? - by taking to bed with you several of the most influential men in the country. One at a time, usually.

PITOU: Madame!

SARAH: Currently you are the mistress of the dashing Duc de Morny.

PITOU: I can't play someone's mistress!

SARAH: It's a game, Pitou! Pretense - the Creator's chief gift! A game to jog the memory under this merciless sun - without my parasol!

PITOU: The parasol, Madame? You need only ask!

(He starts out. She grabs him by the coattails, holds him fast. He turns)

SARAH: Don't make this too difficult for me, Pitou.

(Pause)

PITOU: No, Madame.

SARAH: You begin - MAMAN. Just as we did it before.

PITOU: But, Madame -

SARAH: Please! You are Judith Bernhardt. One of the most ...

PITOU: *(Very quietly)* One of the most ...

SARAH: Glamorous ...

PITOU: *(More quietly)* Glamorous ...

SARAH: Women in Paris.

PITOU: *(A whisper)* ... women in Paris ...

SARAH: That's it!

(Pause. PITOU turns his back on her for a moment, trying to "assume the character." SARAH watches him expectantly)

(In each of his "roles" PITOU remains essentially PITOU, rather ludicrous at first, improving as he goes along. He lightens his voice a bit for Judith and gestures occasionally in what he considers an elegant demimondaine manner, but it is not his favorite, or best, role)

(After a moment he turns around again, as Judith Bernhardt. He has picked up a small ornamental fan from the piano, uses it as a "character prop")

PITOU: *(As Judith Bernhardt)* Mademoiselle Sarah! You are 28 years old!

SARAH: *(Her younger self)* Twenty-SEVEN, Maman.

PITOU: *(Judith)* It's time you left the theater to seek honest employment. You have responsibilities, obligations.

SARAH: *(Sotto voce)* Good, Pitou. *(In the scene)* My obligations are to myself, Maman!

PITOU: *(Judith)* Indeed? And what about -? What about ...?

SARAH: *(Prompting)* What about my baby?

PITOU: *(Judith)* And what about your baby?

SARAH: *(Prompting)* And Prince Henri?

PITOU: *(Judith)* And this fly-by-night Belgian dandy! You don't imagine he'll give your brat a name?

SARAH: *(In the scene)* He loves me, Maman.

PITOU: *(Judith - getting into it more)* Oh, the nobility's always game for a quick backstage tumble, dear. He'll sing a different tune when his parents discover a smear of greasepaint on the family crest!

SARAH: *(Sotto voce)* Wonderful, Pitou! And now she'd start: "I've done my best to -"

PITOU: *(Himself)* I know - I know that bit! *(Judith)* I've done my best to keep us decent. Myself and both my daughters.

SARAH: *(In the scene)* You always cared more for Jeanne! She is your favorite, your pet!

PITOU: *(Judith)* And why not? Jeanne, my baby, my angel. Nervous, yes, but INFINITELY devoted!

SARAH: *(Laughing, out of the scene)* You can't tell me you're not enjoying this, Pitou!

PITOU: *(Himself)* Madame! How can I possibly continue this charade if you -?!

SARAH: I'm sorry! Go on!

(Pause. Again PITOU turns his back on her, "assumes the character.")

PITOU: *(Turning back around, as Judith)* Mademoiselle Sarah, you are the bed of thorns on which my heart rests uneasily! You would never listen, would never let me guide you.

SARAH: *(In the scene)* You wanted Jeanne and me to be perfect replicas of yourself, didn't you, Maman? A Dresden china bitch and her two china whelps!

PITOU: *(Judith)* Don't you dare speak to me like that! You've always been self-willed, impractical! You've always had absurd fantasies about yourself -!

SARAH: Maman -

PITOU: *(Judith)* About life! About MEN! Even when I found you eligible suitors, which was not easy, considering -

SARAH: SUITORS? Is that what they were? I remember - I was 15 when you presented me to that - that hirsute Monsieur Berentz! I'd never seen a man - I'd never seen an ANIMAL so unalterably corporeal! Bristly! He even had hair growing under his fingernails!

PITOU: *(Judith)* He had a fine business.

SARAH: Yes. He made rugs. From his own hair, I have no doubt!

(PITOU-JUDITH gives her a stricken look, turns away, launches into a "mother's soliloquy":)

PITOU: *(Judith)* Doctors usually advise mature women to avoid alcohol, sweets, and any prolonged exercise that might injure the spine. My doctors simply told me to avoid my elder daughter!

SARAH: *(Out of the scene)* That's it! That's Maman! Continue! *(Prompting)* "Naturally I was concerned -"

PITOU: *(Instantly taking the prompt, as Judith)* NATURALLY I was concerned! I am a mother! I saw Sarah evolving into a shrill, rebellious creature with a harsh Semitic profile - which was not really her fault - and a fetish for affectation which her years in the theater did nothing to correct! Far from it. Then, having ruined her own life, she proceeded to - to VULGARIZE my little Jeanne, my baby, my angel, with -

(During this speech, SARAH, her eyes rolling, clasps one hand to her bosom)

SARAH: WAIT!

(PITOU looks at her, uncertain where or who he is)

SARAH: Take this down! Hurry!

(PITOU puts down the fan, races to his notes)

SARAH: Maman - Maman would not let me forget! She blamed me! For Jeanne! For Jeanne's -!

PITOU: Yes? Ready!

SARAH: *(Rapidly)* My sister would say to me, "Sarah, there's a carousel behind my eyes!" And I'd know she was drunk again. Maman blamed me. "Your sister never drank before you adopted her into your theatrical tribe! Before you dragged her off on your insane tours, to New York and God-knows-where-else!" The truth is, I didn't want Jeanne to come. She screamed at me, threatened me. She said I was jealous, afraid she'd show me up to the Americans. So I took her along. Gave her a few small parts, odd jobs. Yes, but we were talking about - about her VULGARIZATION, as you called it, Maman. Her disease. Perhaps it was my fault. I wonder if I ENCOURAGED Jeanne's drinking - looked the other way because - because I hated her? It's a fact! From the beginning I HATED her. Because she was given the best clothes, the holidays, the facial massages with fresh cream!

PITOU: A little slower, Madame!

SARAH: *(No slower)* Jeanne was given every chance! I fought my way into the Conservatoire, fought to stay there! While Maman and her gentlemen laughed at me. But Jeanne -! By some good angel she was given a face that was not a joke. Jeanne was beautiful. Like Maman. You can look like a Jew and be beautiful - or you can look like a Jew and look like a Jew. Jeanne had a nose that was just a nose. She had a mouth. She had hair. I had only my eyes. Everything else I had to INVENT!

PITOU: *(Writing, without looking up)* I can't possibly keep up -!

SARAH: The public EXPECTS beauty! The public expects - EVERY-THING! Beauty and wit -

PITOU: Please, Madame, you're drifting away from -

SARAH: And straight white teeth!

PITOU: From the topic! You were speaking of your sister and her -

SARAH: All my life I have given to the public! I've given them - I've given them ... *(Pause)* Given them what, Maman? Given them what, Pitou?

MEMOIR
John Murrell

Place: as above
Time: late at night, summer, 1922
Characters: Sarah, Pitou

Deep in the night, Sarah struggles against old age, loneliness and fear.
Pitou hears her, comes out onto the terrace, and finds himself in the
middle of a game called "Guess who, Pitou?"

SARAH: WAIT! *(She grabs a stick of black makeup from the case)* Time now
for a NEW game - which we shall call - "Guess Who, Pitou."
*(She hastily draws a thick black line above and below each of her eyes. She
puts her face very close to his, grins hideously)*
SARAH: GUESS WHO, PITOU!
PITOU: Saint Theresa.
SARAH: You're not trying! No, I'm that marvelous mime from the Left
Bank! You know! He was all the rage in the '60s!
PITOU: I wasn't born in the '60s!
SARAH: That clown with the marvelous ugly avian profile, they used
to compare it to mine! YOU KNOW!
PITOU: At this hour I can't even recall my own name!
SARAH: *(Overlapping, suddenly flinging out her arms in birdlike manner)*
LE CORBEAU! Caw, caw, caw! Le Corbeau! Remember?
PITOU: Never heard of him!
SARAH: Caw, caw, caw! LE CORBEAU! And he did that wonderful
routine in which - No, wait! I'll do it for you!
PITOU: *(Rubbing his eyes)* I know I won't recover from this!
SARAH: Le Corbeau's most celebrated routine! *(In a barker's voice)*
Ladies and gentlemen! A chance to see yourselves as others see you!
Le Corbeau will now demonstrate something we ALL love to do!
What? *(She slaps playfully at PITOU, as if he were a wag in the audience)*
No, no, monsieur! It's not THAT! Shame on you! We can't show
THAT onstage! *(She laughs breathlessly, then raises her voice again:)* Le
Corbeau will show us what we spend most of our time doing, all of
us, every day! Watch! See if you recognize what it is!
PITOU: Mother Mary!
SARAH: Ladies and gentlemen! LE CORBEAU!

(She applauds and signals for PITOU to do the same. He applauds, perfunc-torily, unhappily.

Music: a French vaudeville tune, far in the distance. SARAH "makes an entrance," as LE CORBEAU. PITOU watches. She ambles forward a few steps in a lopsided corvine fashion, then seats herself slowly, carefully, on the edge of a chair. She becomes very very still. Pause. And that's it - the whole routine. She merely sits, completely motionless, for a long time. PITOU stares at her, dumbfounded. After at least 20 seconds of total immobility, she glances at him, falls out of the pose. Music fades)

SARAH: Don't you see? They gave him a superb introduction, got the audience so excited! And then - he just sat there! *(She breaks up)* And we laughed - my Jesus!

(She laughs very hard for a moment, then stops, looks at PITOU, who looks back at her blankly)

SARAH: *(As though to a child)* The announcer said, "It's what we spend most of our time doing, all of us!" See?! It's nothing!

PITOU: I understand, Madame. I just don't happen to find it funny.

SARAH: *(Spiteful)* What DO you find funny?

PITOU: At five o'clock in the morning?!

SARAH: If you won't laugh at what I think is funny, then you must have your own THEORY, Pitou, about what is funny and what is not! Let's hear your THEORY!

PITOU: One's sense of humor is personal! I'm not required by my contract to -

SARAH: *(Fiercely)* I have served the public for 55 years! I have made them weep, faint, gasp - and LAUGH! But perhaps YOU, Pitou, can teach ME what people react to, what is really funny!

PITOU: Madame -

SARAH: Your THEORY, Pitou! I'm LISTENING!

(Pause. PITOU thinks it over)

PITOU: *(Flatly)* NOTHING is not funny. SOMETHING is.

(Pause)

SARAH: That's it?

(He nods. She clinches her teeth, snatches a small towel from the makeup case, rubs at the black lines above and below her eyes, smearing them)

SARAH: *(Between her teeth)* Well, what can I expect from Life but IDIOCY? That has become its basic ingredient!

(She throws the towel down, picks up the mirror, stares into it)

SARAH: My God - this isn't a face! It's gray mud. It was a sort of face, before the years began to rain down on it. Now it's only a MUDDY RAG! WITH FIVE HOLES IN IT!

(Using the mirror, she suddenly bats the makeup case off the table. It crashes onto the flagstones. Brushes and little pots of paint scatter across the terrace)

SARAH: It's WORSE than death, Pitou! Inventing these games to pass the night! Holding on - with my teeth and with my nails! - to the games! - now that my real life is over! I'd rather DIE NOW than wait it out!

(Savagely she shoves several handfuls of notes off the table)

PITOU: I knew this would happen!

SARAH: No one listens!

PITOU: I KNEW in five minutes you'd be -

SARAH: That's right, DON'T listen! Shut me out! I want you to shut me out! I did not ASK to pass through this late hour, like an old dream that troubles the sleep of the children! And you are ALL my CHIL-DREN - who cry out to me in the night, "MOTHER!" Not because you need me! But because I TERRIFY you! *(Suddenly very quiet)* Sometimes shapeless - in gray flesh -! I am DYING, Pitou. And I am afraid!

PITOU: Madame Bernhardt! I'm going for the doctor!

SARAH: No!

PITOU: Or Monsieur Maurice!

SARAH: NO!

PITOU:: This madness, it's every night now! It used to be once or twice a month, but NOW -

(She grabs him with one firm hand)

SARAH: Feel how STRONG it is, Pitou! The bone and muscle inside the gray mud! How can THAT die?!

PITOU: Madame!

SARAH: AND I AM NOT MAD!

PITOU: PLEASE!

SARAH: I am not mad YET! UNDERSTAND ME?!

PITOU: NO!

(He pulls free. She slumps back)

PITOU: I'm going - I'm going to fetch your medicine at least!

(He runs into the house. Pause. SARAH looks down at the makeup case, the scattered paints, papers, and so on, all around her. She starts to move away.

All at once she shudders - her entire body shaking. She gasps, stabs one hand into her side, the other into her bosom. She bites her lip, hard. Pause)

SARAH: PITOU ...! *(Pause)* Pitou -? *(She moves forward a little farther. She gasps again, louder. She sways, closes her eyes. Pause. She opens her eyes very wide. A look of anguish crosses her face. She screams hoarsely. She falls. She exhales a long, dry breath. She appears to be dead)*

NURSE JANE GOES TO HAWAII

Allan Stratton

Place: Edgar Chisholm's living room in a Toronto suburb
Time: late afternoon on a Friday; year unspecified; the play was first
   produced in 1980
Characters: Edgar Chisholm, Vivien Bliss

Edgar Chisholm is unhappily married. His wife Doris, a syndicated
   newspaper columnist, does not have much time to spend with him.
   Edgar is convinced that his life is a bore, and he's trying to do
   something about it. A high school geography teacher by day, he has
   enrolled in a night class at the Ontario Institute of Art where he
   spends his evenings making ceramic ashtrays.

While Doris is supposedly away in Windsor doing interviews, Edgar has
   invited Vivien Bliss to spend the weekend at the Chisholm residence.
   Vivien is a writer of trashy romance novels. Desperate to enjoy the
   romantic lifestyle of her heroines, Vivien too is expanding her
   horizons. Having met Edgar in the ceramics class, she now intends
   to have an affair with him. Unbeknown to either of them, however,
   Doris has canceled her Windsor appointments and is in the bathroom, taking a "long hot shower and a good stiff Chivas."

VIVIEN: Why Edgar, it's so ritzy! It's like I always dreamed it would be!
   I mean it's Bungalow City! Oh but I feel wicked.
EDGAR: May I take your coat?
VIVIEN: Not yet. Just let me breathe in the je ne sais quoi. Oh my, an
   Eskimo carving. Did you make it?
EDGAR: Just into ceramics I'm afraid.
VIVIEN: How cruel of me not to notice them first. I spy with my little
   eye something beginning with "ashtray." *(Picks up ceramic)* I remem-

ber when this came out of the kiln. Oh, but I admire your textures. The way they seem to say, "Hello little cigarette, I'm going to hold you in ways you've never dreamed!"

EDGAR: Yes. And there's the typewriter. With Doris in Windsor it's yours for the weekend.

VIVIEN: *(Indicating tape recorder)* Thanks, but I've got Constant Companion. He's taped all my novels and I mustn't be unfaithful. Bad luck. Oh - there's one of your abstracts! *(Goes to woebegone piece of clay)*

EDGAR: Very rough.

VIVIEN: YES! Why, it looks like Hawaii!

EDGAR: Pardon?

VIVIEN: Little volcanoes all over. I can almost see the palm trees.

EDGAR: Doris thinks it should go in the garbage.

VIVIEN: She doesn't even like this one?

EDGAR: When company comes she packs them all up in a box in the basement. Says she doesn't want to see me embarrassed.

VIVIEN: The cad-ess. Why must we artists suffer at such unfeeling hands? Let me comfort. *(She embraces him)*

EDGAR: Vivien.

VIVIEN: *(Releasing)* Oh Edgar, isn't it strange and wonderful and beautiful, the two of us? You, geography teacher by day, artist by night; me, a novelist of passion and romance seeking intrigue; each guided by some Unseen Hand to an extension course in ceramics at the Ontario College of Art! Oh Edgar - *(They are about to kiss)* – I want a drink.

EDGAR: Whiskey Sour?

VIVIEN: You're a psychic!

EDGAR: And would you care for a seat?

VIVIEN: Thank you but no. I'm still exploring this playground of adventure.

EDGAR: Good.

(They blow each other kisses and he exits into the kitchen)

VIVIEN: *(Looks around the room, then says to a ceramic)* Hello "Hawaii." HAWAII! EUREKA! TELEPHONE! BETTY! WHERE'S THE - HAWAII! *(Touchtones furiously, saying)* Ceramics live. They breathe. They - they - oh thank you, Edgar - *(On phone)* Harlequin? This is Vivien Bliss ... Yes, I know my novel was due yesterday. DON'T YELL AT ME, I'M IN PROCESS! Tell Betty I'm luxuriating with my paramour at 16 The Bridle Path. Tell her it's paradise and I'm calling it *Nurse Jane Goes to Hawaii.* I can see it now - lagoons, Ferraris and tsetse flies! Bye! *(Hangs up, to tape recorder) Nurse Jane Goes to Hawaii.* Chapter One. Nurse Jane sighed. Paragraph. She had just arrived in Honolulu from Pleasantville Hospital for an International Symposium on Malaria. And she had met the continental Dr. Edgar Sterling from Britain. He had a strikingly cleft, jutting chin, piercing blue eyes that danced and a

silver tie clip on which was emblazoned his family crest. "Oh, to call him Ed instead of Dr. Sterling," she mused, as they strolled along the shore, listening to the crashing waves while porpoises whistled playfully beyond the coral reef. Paragraph. An agèd denizen approached. "Aloha. You might please to join our luau?" he inquired. Dr. Sterling replied in the affirmative and guided Nurse Jane into the nearby bamboo hut with professional ease. Chapter Two.
(EDGAR re-enters from the kitchen with a tray on which are two Whiskey Sours and a rye bottle)
Suddenly Nurse Jane found herself plied with exotic libations.

EDGAR: Here we are.

VIVIEN: *(To tape)* ..." said Dr. Sterling.

EDGAR: *(Offering drink)* Pardon?

VIVIEN: *(Taking drink, to tape)* "Thank you," she replied huskily.

EDGAR: Vivien?

VIVIEN: *(To tape)* What were his intentions, she pondered with fluttering heart.

EDGAR: Vivien??? *(Touches her)*

VIVIEN: *(To tape)* Dr. Sterling advanced.

EDGAR: Are you all right?

VIVIEN: *(To tape)* "I've never been better," she breathed. An inner voice beckoned. It said –

EDGAR: Are you sure?

VIVIEN: *(Waving him off, to tape)* It said ... *(Turns tape off)* Never mind, it's gone.

EDGAR: Gone?

VIVIEN: *(realizing he doesn't understand)* Sorry. My novel.

EDGAR: I interrupted?!

VIVIEN: It's not your fault. It's ... What can I say?
(Vivien and Edgar clink drink glasses. He sips. Unaccustomed to drinking, she finishes hers in one slow, steady swallow.)

EDGAR: *(beat)* Can I get you anything else?

VIVIEN: *(trying to recover the thread of her novel)* I'm not sure.

EDGAR: Perhaps some music?

VIVIEN: Oh! Love songs!

EDGAR: Perry Como, Herb Alpert, Tony Bennett –

VIVIEN: No, you!

EDGAR: Me?

VIVIEN: Sing to me, Edgar! Put me in the mood. We'll dance while you sing.

EDGAR: Vivien ... have we had a little too much?

VIVIEN: No such thing as too much.

EDGAR: But ...

VIVIEN: Pretty please? For me? Your inspiration? You're so cute when you say that. Come on. *(Vivien sings the first line of a popular romantic upbeat Hawaiian song. She looks expectantly at Edgar who awkwardly* *repeats it. As Vivien exuberantly continues the song, she motions Edgar to sing along, which he attempts to do, repeating the last word or phrase of each line with great emabrrassment in an unintentional parody of an Hawaiian lounge act. As the song builds, Vivien adds "hula-hula dance movements" which Edgar, mortified, attempts to copy. At the song's finale, Vivien hits a a high note and collapses on the couch.)* Gosh, I'm possessed! Thank you.

EDGAR: Vivien ...

VIVIEN: Ah hah? *(Winks)*

EDGAR: I ... look, I'm sorry.

VIVIEN: What about?

EDGAR: This wasn't such a good idea.

VIVIEN: But you sing so well.

EDGAR: Not that. It's just that I've never ... I mean I don't know what I should be doing. I mean, Doris was the first girl I ever dated and what am I saying? I was married once before for heaven's sake. To my first wife, Betty.But that was a whirlwind affair, a matter of weeks, actually, because of my ... habit. I was obsessed with Atmospheric Optics - reams of charts and statistics which Betty would throw in the air –

VIVIEN: Say no more. My editor's a Betty too, and she's a terror.

EDGAR: Forget your editor. Forget Betty. What I'm trying to say is - I feel like a fool.

VIVIEN: Why?

EDGAR: Never mind. I'll drive you home.

VIVIEN: But you said we'd have the weekend. You promised and I've told Harlequin I'm here and - oh Edgar, this weekend means so much to me!

EDGAR: You don't have to pretend.

VIVIEN: But I want to pretend. And with you. All weekend. Passion, desire, romance ... *(Pause)* It's something I've done, isn't it? I've done something.

EDGAR: No, no, you've been delightful. It's me.

VIVIEN: You don't have to lie. I always do something. Always. I meet someone really interesting, a kindred spirit, someone I love who I think loves me - and I meet them everywhere: at weaving class, pottery class, life drawing class - my life is class after class after class. And it always ends up the same. I get in the door having a wonderful time, thinking we're getting along famously, and all of a sudden I'm back in the car being driven home and he won't even look at me. And I let myself in and go up to my bedsitter, praying Miss Clement won't ask how the date went - and she keeps her hearing aid low so you practically have to SCREAM "I failed again" to all the neighbors - and I go into my room and rummage about in my hope chest, through quilts, linen, stitch-work - or maybe just stare at the one corsage I ever got to press in my Bible. And I have a good cry. Because I don't know what I've done - they never say. And it must be me because it's always the same. Then I pull out a Kleenex and turn on the tape and talk about Nurse Jane and her exciting adventures. And it's not fair! I'm a virgin, damnit, and it's not fair! Of course so is Nurse Jane - but at least she gets more than a parting embrace! *(She turns away)*

EDGAR: *(Quietly)* Vivien ... I'm sorry.

VIVIEN: Don't tell me you're sorry. I'm tired of people saying they're sorry. Do you have a subway token?

EDGAR: No, Vivien, no.

VIVIEN: That's okay. I can hitch-hike. *(Goes to the front door)*

EDGAR: No Vivien, please - stay with me?

VIVIEN: Very good of you, but I don't need mercy. And besides, the linen needs ironing.

EDGAR: Vivien, I ... Look at me? ... Vivien? *(She does)* Stay with me? Please?

VIVIEN: *(Throws herself in his arms)* Oh Edgar!

EDGAR: I thought you thought I was a boring old fool.

VIVIEN: Edgar, you're the most marvelous man I ever met.

EDGAR: And make sure you catch Miss Clement in the hall Sunday night.

VIVIEN: "I did it Miss Clement! I did it!"

EDGAR: *(as Miss Clement)* "Eh?"

VIVIEN: "I'm a fallen woman at last!"

EDGAR: "Oooooo."

(They laugh)

VIVIEN: Edgar?

EDGAR: Yes?

VIVIEN: You will see me after this weekend, won't you? I mean, you will call me?

EDGAR: Forever.

VIVIEN: Oh Edgar.

EDGAR: Yes?

VIVIEN: Let's have some wine.

EDGAR: On top of Whiskey Sours?

VIVIEN: Absolutely. Let's make tonight a celebration - of life and earth and us.

EDGAR: And your novel.

VIVIEN: Oh yes.

EDGAR: Red or white, what's your fancy?

VIVIEN: Who cares? Something grand but simple.

EDGAR: Elemental without being tawdry?

VIVIEN: Oh my, do you mind if I steal that?

EDGAR: I'd be flattered.

VIVIEN: Nurse Jane can exclaim it in a tornado! Are there tornadoes in Hawaii?

EDGAR: No. *(VIVIEN turns away disappointed)* Tropical cyclones, though.

VIVIEN: You're a Godsend!

EDGAR: They come with the trade winds - your basic Trade Wind Littoral Climate under the Koeppen Classification.

VIVIEN: And when they hit little Hawaii - look out!

EDGAR: Yes.

VIVIEN: Tell me more.

EDGAR: I'm not boring you?

VIVIEN: Lord, no! Go on, go on!

EDGAR: Well - *(He beams, then professorially)* we start with moist, warm air ...

VIVIEN: Moist, warm air.

EDGAR: Yes. In a low-pressure area. With easy convection. Now a drop in this pressure - no matter how slight - starts the moist warm air circling or spinning ...

VIVIEN: Or gyrating madly?

EDGAR: Exactly. Nice phrase.

VIVIEN: I use it a lot.

EDGAR: But as moisture condenses in the convection column, the updraft of air speeds up, gyrating even more madly.

VIVIEN: With passionate abandon?

EDGAR: Yes! And our air pressure lowers uniformly toward the vortex of our tropical cyclone. And how do we know our air pressure is lowering uniformly?

VIVIEN: How??

EDGAR: By observing the concentric pattern of isobars!! *(In flight)* And there's so much more to discover!! The influence of jet streams, for example. Do tongues of polar air at high altitudes sweep south, pulling or dragging lower air with them as the axis turns, pressing northward?? God, but it's a motherlode of intrigue to the initiated! But to the wine. "Farewell my love," he said. "I'm off to stalk the wine cellar." *(He picks up the drink tray)*

VIVIEN: Hooray! Oh, don't clear that. *(Takes rye bottle off tray)*

EDGAR: With wine?

VIVIEN: Of course not, silly. After. *(Puts it under the couch)* Let's hide it under the ceremonial altar for a surprise nightcap. Like pirates and buried treasure. *(Whispers)* Shhh. X marks the spot.

EDGAR: Ahar matie. *(Lifts one leg in imitation of Long John Silver)* When I get back I'll give you all the dirt on Atmospheric Optics.

VIVIEN: Aloha. *(Blows him a kiss, which he catches)*

EDGAR: Aloha. *(Blows her a kiss, which she catches. He exits with the tray down the corridor)*

VIVIEN: *(To tape)* Dr. Sterling left to find her a bottle of Maui wine, perhaps squeezed by the same brown toes that surrounded her now. "Pray he be not carried out to sea in the embrace of a passionately gyrating typhoon," she breathed.

ODD JOBS

Frank Moher

Place: the Arends' dining room, Edmonton
Time: evening, the present
Characters: Tim Arends, late twenties; his wife Ginette; Mrs. Phipps, in her seventies

At the beginning of the play, Tim Arends loses his job as a welder in an Edmonton factory; he is replaced by a machine. He decides to look for other employment but finds that, without high school matriculation, he is generally underqualified. One day, out of a desire to be useful and to make some money, he offers to look after his neighbor's yard.

Tim's neighbor Mrs. Phipps is a retired mathematics professor. She is having a difficult time coming to terms with old age and with a mind that drifts off, occasionally, to relive the distant past. She is still capable, in lucid moments, of explaining Standell's theorem, but she is alarmed by her propensity to act irrationally—earlier in the play, she reports that she awoke one morning to find herself lying in a ditch next to the freeway.

The following scene occurs after dinner, in the Arend home. Mrs. Phipps and Tim have become friends, and he begins to feel a responsibility to help her through the difficulties she is experiencing. But Tim's wife Ginette, a transplanted Quebecois, is interested in moving on. She sees her job (answering telephones at Sears) as a dead-end, and she has convinced Tim—or so she thinks— that he should move with her to Regina, where she will have the opportunity to work with computers. However, Tim is not really committed to this plan, and he has not explained it to Mrs. Phipps.

Country music. MRS. PHIPPS and GINETTE are listening. They are in TIM and GINETTE's house.
MRS. PHIPPS: *(After a while)* You really like this, do you?
GINETTE: Love it.
MRS. PHIPPS: I don't know. It's too ... SOMETHING for me.
GINETTE: You ever been Done Wrong, Mrs. Phipps?

MRS. PHIPPS: Done What?

GINETTE: Wrong. Country music is for people who been Done Wrong.

MRS. PHIPPS: Oh. Well obviously I haven't.

GINETTE: Well I have. I thought I was marrying a cowboy. And look what I got. The Galloping Gourmet.

MRS. PHIPPS: Is he still in the kitchen?

GINETTE: Still in the kitchen. He's been in there all day.
(Pause. Music plays. GINETTE and MRS. PHIPPS listen, mellow)

MRS. PHIPPS: *(After a pause)* Did you really?

GINETTE: Hmm?

MRS. PHIPPS: Think you were marrying a cowboy.

GINETTE: I did. Well that's what I came to Alberta to do. And Tim seemed like the real thing. He had a foam rubber Stetson and a belt-buckle so big he couldn't sit down. *(Pause)* I remember I met him at Danny Hooper's. Where I'd gone to meet cowboys. He told me he had a 25-acre spread just outside of town. And an Eldorado Cadillac with a pair of bull-horns mounted on the grille. I didn't believe him of course. But I did a little bit. If you know what I mean. *(Pause)* Anyway. That's how I got all my records. When it turned out he wasn't a cowboy, he started buying me cowboy records instead. Ronnie Milsap. Merle Haggard. The Burritto Brothers, they were popular then. I have exactly 442 cowboy records! No! Four hundred and forty-SIX, if you count the boxed set as four. *(Wry smile)* My sisters still think I'm married to a cowboy. So what. I just let them dream.

MRS. PHIPPS: It sounds like it runs in your family.

GINETTE: I guess so. Or maybe I was just dumber than I am now.
(Pause)

MRS. PHIPPS: I came out into the yard yesterday and your husband was dressed up in Wendell's old climbing gear. The old flannel shirt, the pick, the rope slung over his shoulder. I hadn't seen any of it in years. I just dragged it all into the garage the day after his funeral, locked it up and threw the key on top of the china cabinet. I must say he looked grand. I gave his cap a little pull. That's what I used to do for Wendell, give the brim a little tug for good luck.

GINETTE: Well, you should have given him the boot and sent him home.

MRS. PHIPPS: Hmm?

GINETTE: All the time he spends at your place.

MRS. PHIPPS: I hope you don't mind?

GINETTE: Mrs. Phipps. I'm just glad he gets up in the morning.

MRS. PHIPPS: Ah.

GINETTE: TIM! IF YOU'RE SERVING DESSERT LET'S DO IT BEFORE SUNDAY! *(To MRS. PHIPPS)* That ought to get him. He hates it when I yell.

(TIM enters with dessert)

TIM: Hold yer horses, hold yer horses. Good food takes time. *(Handing out desserts)* One for you. And one for you. If you don't like it, pretend like you do.

GINETTE: What is it?

TIM: Raspberry Frappe.
(GINETTE and MRS. PHIPPS groan)
What's the matter?

GINETTE: Raspberries!

TIM: What about 'em?

MRS. PHIPPS: I think we've been raspberried out.

TIM: Well I tell ya what, I only got six or seven jars left. Then I'm movin' into apples. Flo says the Macs are comin' in.

GINETTE: Who's Flo?

TIM: She's the store manager at the Safeway.

MRS. PHIPPS: Where DOES he find the time to do all this?

TIM: Time is all in your head, Mrs. Phipps. See, that's the thing I'm learnin'. You got time for whatever you want to have time for. *(Beat)* Well hey! Couple of pretty fillies like you. Watcha say we get in the Oldsmobile and hit the town?

GINETTE: And do what?

TIM: I dunno. Go drinkin', dancing.

MRS. PHIPPS: We could get started on your math lessons tonight.

GINETTE: What math lessons?

MRS. PHIPPS: His math lessons. I'm going to help him out.

TIM: *(Quickly)* Yeah, we could do that Mrs. Phipps, uh, why doncha finish up yer frappe there, there we go. Make some room for a second helping. *(Eating)* Yea, y'know the thing is you gotta put in just the right amount of brandy. First time I tried it, that was all you could taste. *(Pause)* Tell you what, Ginette, you go get the cards and we'll get a round of Crazy Eights happenin' here.

GINETTE: Oh! Crazy Eights! I hate that game!

MRS. PHIPPS: I've never played it.

GINETTE: Tim LOVES it.

TIM: I don't LOVE it. I just happen to be very good at it.

GINETTE: That's Tim's idea of a good Friday night. Sitting down and beating me at cards.

TIM: Yeah, that's right. Take all 'er money off 'er. 'Course I have to give it back next morning, eh, so's she can buy me my Wheaties.

GINETTE: Ha!

TIM: Go on, Ginette, go get the cards.

GINETTE: I can't.

TIM: I won't beat ya.

GINETTE: I packed them.

MRS. PHIPPS: You packed them?

GINETTE: Yes. I wanted to get the small stuff done first.

MRS. PHIPPS: Are you ... going somewhere?

GINETTE: *(Confused)* YES. To REGINA, Mrs. Phipps.

MRS. PHIPPS: Oh. For how long?

(Beat)

GINETTE: Tim -

TIM: Uh, yeah, listen, we can talk about that tomorrow. Why don't I go get the cards? Oh yeah. I can't ... do that.

(Pause)

GINETTE: You didn't tell her?

TIM: Leave it, Ginny, just leave it.

MRS. PHIPPS: Tell me what?

GINETTE: Mrs. Phipps, Tim and I are MOVING to Regina. I got a job there, I thought you knew.

MRS. PHIPPS: Oh. Oh yes. Regina. I see.

TIM: You just had to do that, huh Ginny?

GINETTE: Tim didn't tell you?

TIM: YOU JUST HAD TO DO THAT, HUH?

MRS. PHIPPS: Oh well yes he TOLD me! He TOLD me, of course! I just meant to say - WHEN are you going? I knew you were going, of course, but WHEN are you going, that's what I need to know.

TIM: It's all right, Mrs. Phipps.

MRS. PHIPPS: Because I'll have to make plans, you see, I'll have to make some plans -

TIM: MRS. PHIPPS, IT'S ALL RIGHT.

MRS. PHIPPS: Because Regina is a very lovely city, Regina is where ... yes, that's right. Regina is where Wendell goes all the time, on conferences. I've never been there myself, but he tells me about it, he knows all the Indians there, or something, they've made him an honorary Indian chief, I think. *(Pause)* I think it's Regina.

GINETTE: I'll get her coat.

TIM: Ginny -

GINETTE: I think you should go home now, Mrs. Phipps.

TIM: She'll be all right. Now we're finishing our dessert and then we'll -

GINETTE: Let go of me -

TIM: I'm not -

GINETTE: LET GO OF ME! I DON'T WANT YOUR GODDAMN DESSERT! *(Pause)* Why didn't you tell her?

TIM: I don't know.

GINETTE: Because you thought I would -

TIM: BECAUSE I DON'T KNOW, MAYBE I'LL GO THERE, MAYBE I WON'T. MAYBE YOU'LL GO THERE, MAYBE I'LL STAY HERE. I don't KNOW yet, so how can I tell her when I don't even know?

GINETTE: You don't know yet.

TIM: No.

GINETTE: Well you rented the goddamn U-Haul.

TIM: I KNOW I rented the U-Haul, because I THOUGHT I was going, but how can I go, <u>LOOK</u> AT HER, HOW CAN I GO? So you go, I'll stay here, and I'll come later, or something like that, WHAT THE HELL CAN I DO? WHADDA YOU WANT ME TO DO? *(Pause)* So you go. And I'll come later. C'mon MRS. PHIPPS, your coat is in the hall. *(Pause)*

GINETTE: You want me to tell them no, don't you?

TIM: I'm telling you nothing.

GINETTE: You want me to go to Sears and tell them it was all a big mistake. 'Please Mrs. Gibbons, can I still answer phones for you, and listen to angry people all day, and listen to people call me a BITCH?' It makes me SICK, it makes me SICK that job, I go in and just the sound of a phone is enough to make me ill. And you want me to stay? Well you can go to hell. Because I'm not staying in a job like that. *(Pause)*

MRS. PHIPPS: Clo? Chloe? Come out and look at the sun. Do you have your camera, Chloe? It's just starting to rise. *(Pause)* Daisy's Dragon. Hiberian Fireweed. No, a One-eyed Jack's Purse, I think. That's what it is. *(Pause)* Ten. To the power of two. To the power of 13. To the power of 29. *(Pause)* Oh. Oh! Now! Perfect! Now! Oh, the sun! Did you get it Chloe? Did you bring your camera? LOOK at it Chloe! The sun! The sun!

(MRS. PHIPPS spreads her arms, as if to embrace the light. She presses her palms to her face, then opens her arms wide again, as if to soak up the light. She stands there with her arms open. TIM and GINETTE watch)

PLAY MEMORY

Joanna M. Glass

Place: Miss Halverson's office at the school, Saskatoon
Time: 1954
Characters: Jean, 12 years old; Miss Halverson

Play Memory is about one family as seen through the eyes of the
daughter and only child, Jean. Jean's father Cam was once a promi-
nent salesman with Havilland Tobacco. The company, however,
considered him too much of a maverick. When it became known
that Havilland salesmen were systematically swapping tobacco for
gas ration coupons (in wartime), the company decided to use Cam
as a scapegoat. He lost his job and his dignity; he became a rather
violent alcoholic.

Several years later, Jean's mother Ruth is forced to work outside the
home because Cam can no longer hold down a job. When Ruth is at
home, she spends a good deal of time protecting Jean from Cam's
vitriolic outbursts. Jean has developed a bladder problem which
makes it difficult for her to conduct herself gracefully at school. She
is a troubled child, and the guidance councilor Miss Halverson
attempts to help her. Later in the play, when Cam's violence
becomes unbearable, Miss Halverson will be instrumental in moving
Jean and Ruth out of Cam's house.

*The lights come up on MISS HALVERSON's office. She is a woman of 30,
humane and caring. There may be two photographs on a wall and one large
print. The photos are of King George VI, and Winston Churchill. The print
is of a painting by Tom Thomson, one of the "Canadian Seven." MISS
HALVERSON rises from her desk, as JEAN enters.*
HALVERSON: Good morning, Jean.
JEAN: *(She is distraught. She tries, heroically, to control herself)* Good
morning.
HALVERSON: *(Gesturing)* Please, sit down.

JEAN: No. *(Pause)* Thank you.

HALVERSON: *(Embarrassed, hesitating)* You're ... wet.

JEAN: Yes. I've had an accident. I really must go home.

HALVERSON: This is the 2nd accident in class, Jean. And your grade-school records show it was a problem there, too. I think we have to talk about some medical attention.

JEAN: No! *(She tries to maintain her calm)* The doctor knows my troubles. I - only wet when I'm hit.

HALVERSON: But you were in Home-Ec last period, Jean. No one hits you in Home-Ec.

JEAN: I got - confused, for a moment.

HALVERSON: Can you explain that?

JEAN: There was a lot of noise in the class. A lot of girls, arguing, and lots of machines, running. And I - mistook it, you see. I got scared.

HALVERSON: Yes?

JEAN: And then Miss Pendleton lifted a yardstick over my head. I'm sorry. I know it doesn't make sense. I thought she was going to hit me, and I wet. *(Pause)* I don't understand it. Usually, see, it's here - *(She gestures)* - in the lower back.

HALVERSON: Where you're hit.

JEAN: Yes.

HALVERSON: But last year, when I called you in, you had a large crescent on your cheek. I think you weren't truthful then, Jean. You said you fell on an opened tobacco can. You said the rim caused the mark.

JEAN: Yes. He has to roll his own nowadays. So the can was open *(She sees HALVERSON's disbelief)* It was thrown.

HALVERSON: It would have to be thrown with some force, to leave such a contusion.

JEAN: *(Relenting)* It was shoved. Against my face. *(Pause: a note of hope)* But he doesn't do that anymore. My mum says a woman's face is her calling card.

HALVERSON: Why does he hit you, Jean?

JEAN: He's very unhappy. He was fired, you see, and disgraced.

HALVERSON: That was 1944, Jean. Ten years ago.

JEAN: He says he hates my smell. I sometimes smell of fish from - *(Catching herself)* - a place I go on the weekend.

HALVERSON: I won't ask about that. You're underage.

JEAN: Yes, Thank you.

HALVERSON: Does he hit your mother?

JEAN: No. Well -

HALVERSON: Yes?

JEAN: *(Tears begin. She tries not to break down)* He ... last week ... burned her arm.

HALVERSON: How?

JEAN: *(Her temper flares, but at her plight, rather than at HALVERSON)* You don't KNOW, you see. You don't know when you're safe, so you're always walking on eggs. You just can't gauge his moods. She put a fresh teapot down in front of him and he jumped up and threw it at her. It was scalding hot, and she had a thick sweater on, so it stuck. 'Til we unbuttoned it and pulled it off.

HALVERSON: *(Goes to her with a couple of Kleenex tissues. She touches JEAN's shoulder, gently, and gestures to the chair)* Please sit down. Really, it's all right. *(JEAN sits; HALVERSON moves behind the desk)* Had she angered him?

JEAN: No. She has an odor, too, you see, from lard. She makes pies where she works. He can't stand our working smells. He says we smell "menial." *(She pauses, and inhales deeply)* What you have to understand, Miss Halverson, is that my mother loves him. They go at each other something terrible, but she loves him.

HALVERSON: I understand that.

JEAN: *(Quizzically, rather daringly)* Do you?

HALVERSON: *(Smiling)* I think your disbelief comes from my "Miss."

JEAN: Well -

HALVERSON: I was engaged to a man once. He was killed at Dieppe. August 19, 1942.

JEAN: I'm very sorry.

HALVERSON: Three thousand Canadians, you know, lost at Dieppe. *(There is a brief silence between them)* Well. Your father refuses to work?

JEAN: Oh, I don't think he could, now. He talks to himself. And he imagines things. Vermin. Parasites. He's lost all of his books, so he goes to the library sometimes. Sneaks over there, just before closing time. He hardly ever goes out during the day.

HALVERSON: Why?

JEAN: He's embarrassed about his clothing. He's ashamed of his appearance.

HALVERSON: *(Settling back, examining JEAN's face)* Jean, do you know the main difference between humans and animals?

JEAN: *(Thinking)* Well, we - walk - upright -

HALVERSON: We think. We have choices. We're very lucky that we live in a free society. Our boys died for that. No matter how bad things may get, we are human, and we do have alternatives. Remember that, will you?

JEAN: Yes, Miss Halverson, I will.

THE REZ SISTERS

Tomson Highway

Place: Wasaychigan Hill Indian Reserve, Manitoulin Island, Ontario; the roof of Pelajia Patchnose's house
Time: a beautiful day in late August, 1986
Characters: Pelajia Patchnose, 53; Philomena Moosetail, 49

Pelajia Patchnose and her sister Philomena Moosetail are looking for a change of scenery. Pelajia is tired of the dirt roads on the reserve; she longs to go to Toronto, to its paved streets, and to her sons who live there. Philomena's aspirations are closer to home; she wants to buy a big, wide, very white toilet. Shingling Pelajia's roof one day, they conceive a plan to win a bingo jackpot—a plan that will eventually lead them to Toronto and to the biggest bingo in the world.

PELAJIA: PHILOMENA. I wanna go to Toronto.
PHILOMENA: *(From offstage)* Oh, go on.
PELAJIA: Sure as I'm sitting away up here on the roof of this old house. I kind of like it up here, though. From here, I can see half of Manitoulin Island on a clear day. I can see the chimneys, the tops of apple trees, the garbage heap behind Big Joey's dumpy little house. I can see the seagulls circling over Marie-Adele Starblanket's white picket fence. Boats on the North Channel I wish I was on, sailing away somewhere. The mill at Espanola, a hundred miles away .. and that's with just a bit of squinting. See? If I had binoculars, I could see the superstack in Sudbury. And if I were Superwoman, I could see the CN Tower in Toronto. Ah, but I'm just plain old Pelajia Rosella Patchnose and I'm here in plain, dusty, boring old Wasaychigan Hill ... Wasy ... waiting ... waiting ... nailing shining shingles with my trusty silver hammer on the roof of Pelajia Rosella Patchnose's little two-bedroom welfare house. Philomena. I wanna go to Toronto.
(PHILOMENA Moosetail comes up the ladder to the roof with one shingle and obviously hating it. She is very well-dressed, with a skirt, nylons, even heels, completely impractical for the roof)

PHILOMENA: Oh, go on.

PELAJIA: I'm tired, Philomena, tired of this place. There's days I wanna leave so bad.

PHILOMENA: But you were born here. All your poop's on this reserve.

PELAJIA: Oh, go on.

PHILOMENA: You'll never leave.

PELAJIA: Yes, I will. When I'm old.

PHILOMENA: You're old right now.

PELAJIA: I got a good 30 years to go ...

PHILOMENA: ... and you're gonna live every one of them right here beside me ...

PELAJIA: ... maybe 40 ...

PHILOMENA: ... here in Wasy. *(Tickles PELAJIA on the breasts)* Chiga-chiga-chiga.

PELAJIA: *(Yelps and slaps PHILOMENA's hand away)* Oh, go on. It's not like it used to be.

PHILOMENA: Oh, go on. People change, places change, time changes things. You expect to be young and gorgeous forever?

PELAJIA: See? I told you I'm not old.

PHILOMENA: Oh, go on. You.

PELAJIA: "Oh, go on. You." You bug me like hell when you say that.

PHILOMENA: You say it, too. And don't give me none of this "I don't like this place. I'm tired of it." This place is too much inside your blood. You can't get rid of it. And it can't get rid of you.

PELAJIA: Four thirty this morning, I was woken by ...

PHILOMENA: Here we go again.

PELAJIA: ... Andrew Starblanket and his brother, Matthew. Drunk. Again. Or sounded like ...

PHILOMENA: Nothing better to do.

PELAJIA: ... fighting over some girl. Heard what sounded like a baseball bat landing on somebody's back. My lawn looks like the shits this morning.

PHILOMENA: Well, I like it here. Myself, I'm gonna go to every bingo and I'm gonna hit every jackpot between here and Espanola and I'm gonna buy me that toilet I'm dreaming about at night ... big and wide and very white ...

PELAJIA: Aw-ni-gi-naw-ee-dick.[1]

PHILOMENA: I'm good at bingo.

PELAJIA: So what! And the old stories, the old language. Almost all gone ... was a time Nanabush and Windigo and everyone here could rattle away in Indian fast as Bingo Betty could lay her bingo chips down on a hot night.

---

1 Oh, go on. *(Ojibway)*

PHILOMENA: Pelajia Rosella Patchnose. The sun's gonna drive you crazy. *(And she descends the ladder)*

PELAJIA: Everyone here's crazy. No jobs. Nothing to do but drink and screw each other's wives and husbands and forget about our Nanabush. *(From offstage PHILOMENA screams. She fell down the ladder)* Philomena! *(As she looks over the edge of the roof)* What are you doing down there?

PHILOMENA: What do you think? I fell.

PELAJIA: Bring me some of them nails while you're down there.

PHILOMENA: *(Whining and still from offstage, from behind the house)* You think I can race up and down this ladder? You think I got wings?

PELAJIA: You gotta wear pants when you're doing a man's job. See? You got your skirt ripped on a nail and now you can see your thighs. People gonna think you just came from Big Joey's house.

PHILOMENA: *(She comes up the ladder in a state of disarray)* Let them think what they want. That old cow Gazelle Nataways ... always acting like she thinks she's still a spring chicken. She's got them legs of hers wrapped around Big Joey day and night ...

PELAJIA: Philomena. Park your tongue. My old man has to go the hundred miles to Espanola just to get a job. My boys. Gone to Toronto. Only place educated Indian boys can find decent jobs these days. And here I sit all broken-hearted.

PHILOMENA: Paid a dime and only farted.

PELAJIA: Look at you. You got dirt all over your backside. *(Turning her attention to the road in front of her house and standing up for the first and only time)* And dirt roads! Years now that old chief's been making speeches about getting paved roads "for my people" and still we got dirt roads all over.

PHILOMENA: Oh, go on.

PELAJIA: When I win me that jackpot next time we play bingo in Espanola ...

PHILOMENA: *(Examining her torn skirt, her general state of disarray, and fretting over it)* Look at this! Will you look at this! Ohhh!

PELAJIA: ... I'm gonna put that old chief to shame and build me a nice paved road right here in front of my house. Jet black. Shiny. Make my lawn look real nice.

PHILOMENA: My rib-cage!

PELAJIA: And if that old chief don't wanna make paved roads for all my sisters around here ...

PHILOMENA: There's something rattling around inside me!

PELAJIA: ... I'm packing my bags and moving to Toronto. *(Sits down again)*

PHILOMENA: Oh, go on.

(She spies Annie Cook's approach a distance up the hill)

Why, I do believe that cloud of dust over there is Annie Cook racing down the hill, Pelajia.

PELAJIA: Philomena. I wanna go to Toronto.

PHILOMENA: She's walking mighty fast. Must be excited about something.

PELAJIA: Never seen Annie Cook walk slow since the day she finally lost Eugene to Marie-Adele at the church 19 years ago. And even then she was walking a little too fast for a girl who was supposed to be broken-heart ... *(Stopping just in time and laughing)* ... heart-broken.

SALT-WATER MOON

David French

Place: the front porch of Mrs. Dawe's house, Newfoundland
Time: "a lovely night in August 1926"
Characters: Mary Snow, 17; Jacob Mercer, 18

Jacob Mercer returns home to Newfoundland from Toronto, where he
has been seeking his fortune for the past year. He is "fresh off the
train"; he arrives at Mrs. Dawe's house, where Mary is in service as a
maid, carrying "a cardboard suitcase held together with a rope tied
in a half-hitch knot."

A year ago, Mary and Jacob were sweethearts. But Jacob's departure to
Toronto was sudden and unexplained (he left to avoid embarrass-
ment after his father was cruelly exploited by Will MacKenzie, local
merchant and employer). The intervening year has been, for Mary,
a time of trying to forget Jacob. She has recently become engaged to
Will MacKenzie's son Jerome, a 20 year-old high school teacher. The
wealth of the MacKenzie family is an allurement for Mary; if she
marries Jerome, she will have a house of her own and no need of
outside employment.

Intent on regaining Mary's affections this late in the day, Jacob must
be quick-witted and resourceful. He scoffs at Jerome's learnedness, at
his myopia, at his claim that baldness is a sign of potency. He
presents Mary with two pairs of silk stockings, bought in Toronto. At
one point, having inspired Mary's wrath, he promises to leave the
yard if she shows him the Star of Vega. He uses the ploy to get closer
to her and then, of course, reneges on his promise to leave.

There is an urgency behind Jacob's wooing in the following scene and
throughout the play: Mary is to be wedded next month, and Jerome
has promised to drop by later this same evening.

JACOB: Do you love him?

MARY: What odds to you? He's a good man, Jerome. He's quiet and kind, he's smart and dependable, and once he builds his own house in Country Road, we're taking Dot to live with us.

JACOB: That's not what I asked, Mary. He may be all of those t'ings you said, and more. I don't give a damn if he's wise like Solomon or strong like Samson. I don't care if he builds 10 houses in Country Road for you and your sister. I only asked if you loved him.

MARY: Why wouldn't I love him? I'm marrying him, aren't I? *(She turns away)*

JACOB: That still don't answer my question. Look at me, Mary ...

MARY: What for? ...

JACOB: Look me in the eye and tell me you loves him, and I'll walk out of this yard and never come back.

MARY: You made one promise tonight you never kept. You can't be trusted.

JACOB: Try me once more. Tell me you loves Jerome McKenzie, and you'll never see the dust of my feet again.

MARY: All right, and I'm holding you to it. *(She turns and stares straight at him)*
(Slight pause)

JACOB: You can't say it, can you? *(Then)* Can you?

MARY: I loves him. There. I said it.

JACOB: *(Beat)* No odds. I don't believe you. *(He walks away)*

MARY: No, you wouldn't believe the Devil if he snuck up behind and jabbed you with his fork.

JACOB: That I wouldn't.

MARY: No. All you believes is what you wants to believe.

JACOB: No, I believes in what's real. I believes in flesh and blood. I believes in a young girl trembling at my breath on her neck. That's what I believes in.

MARY: What young girl?

JACOB: There's only one in the yard that I can see.

MARY: And just when was I trembling?

JACOB: When? I'll tell you when. When you pointed out the blue star of Vega tonight, and I stood behind you. I could feel you shaking under your dress like a young bride at the altar.

MARY: It's chilly out!

JACOB: Indeed it's not chilly out, or where's your shawl to? ... Your heart was pounding, wasn't it? *(Then)* Wasn't it?

MARY: Next you'll be telling me you could hear it.

JACOB: No, but I could see the pulse in your neck, Mary, beating like a tom-tom.

MARY: The Bible's got it all wrong. It's not the women who are the vain ones, it's the men.

(Slight pause)

JACOB: You ought to wear yellow more often, maid. It really do become you. Suits your black hair and fair complexion.

MARY: Is that what you did the past year up in Toronto? Sweet talk the girls?

JACOB: What girls?

MARY: "What girls?" he says.

JACOB: There wasn't any girls, sure.

MARY: No, and autumn don't follow summer, I suppose?

JACOB: *(Beat)* All right, perhaps there was one or two girls ...

MARY: One or two? Is THAT all?

JACOB: T'ree or four at most.

MARY: You don't need to exaggerate. And you calls Jerome a blowhard for boasting of somet'ing he never claimed to be in the first place?

JACOB: He claimed to be potent, didn't he?

MARY: That's all he claimed to be, not'ing more. And he said it as a joke, more or less.

JACOB: More or less?

MARY: I'm sorry I ever told you, now.

JACOB: He's in the wrong place, Jerome is. He ought to try Toronto. The girls up there haven't set eyes on a decent man since the day I left.

MARY: Yes, and I suppose all four was waving you off at the station? Running down the tracks? Blowing you kisses? "Don't forget us, now! Come back soon!"

JACOB: No. Only the two.

MARY: Two, my foot.

JACOB: All right, one then. One in particular.

MARY: Oh?

JACOB: Her name was Rose, and she looked like you. In fact, she might've been your spitting image, except for her gentle manner.

MARY: *(Beat)* I'm gentle ...

JACOB: The odd time.

MARY: I'm not like this with another soul but you. I've never met anyone who makes me cross as a hornet half the time.

JACOB: Rose was gentle ALL the time. She said I brought out the best in her.

MARY: There was no Rose. You're making it up. What was her last name?

JACOB: I'm not much with last names. Rose of Sharon, I called her. "How beautiful are thy feet with shoes, O prince's daughter!" ...

MARY: *(Beat)* What did you do together, you and this ... this Rose?

JACOB: Oh, the odd time we'd go dancing at the Palace Pier. That's a dancehall down by Lake Ontario. Once we took a midnight cruise to Niagara Falls and back. There was a band playing.

MARY: I don't believe a word of it.

JACOB: Mostly we'd go to a picture show. My favorite *(Last syllable rhymes with "night")* was always Tom Mix.

MARY: Tom Mix? Who in the world is he?

JACOB: What? You've never heard of the "King of the Cowboys," the most famous Western actor alive?

MARY: No, and I still haven't seen a picture show. I don't have the time or money for such t'ings.

JACOB: Then I'll take you, maid! Right now!

MARY: Take me where?

JACOB: To the pictures, Mary. I'll take you to see Tom Mix in "The Lucky Horseshoe." *(He sits on the step and pats the area beside him)* Here. Sit down on the step.

MARY: *(Suspiciously)* What's you up to now?

JACOB: *(All innocence)* I'm not up to a blessed t'ing ...
(MARY still regards him with mistrust)
... Come on, sit down. I won't bite ... Will you hurry up, we'll be late for the picture ...
(MARY reluctantly sits down, though she sits at a discreet distance from JACOB)
... All right, now it's a Friday night in Toronto, and we'm at the picture house. We just slipped into the last row of the Christie T'eater on St. Clair. You comfortable?

MARY: Yes. Only why are we sitting so far back? Why don't we sit in the front?

JACOB: Why? 'Cause all the front seats are taken, that's why. Jesus, we just sat down, and already you'm complaining.

MARY: I just wondered why we had to sit in the last row.

JACOB: I told you, didn't I? These are the only two seats left. Count yourself lucky to get 'em ... All right, now, the next is important. There are t'ree t'ings, MARY, that a fellow who takes his sweetheart -

MARY: I'm not your sweetheart.

JACOB: Suit yourself.

MARY: Just remember that.

JACOB: Hush up. The picture's about to begin ... No, it's just the newsreel ... Now as I was saying, there are t'ree t'ings that a fellow who takes a girl to the pictures always does in a picture house. And if he don't do all t'ree to his satisfaction, he don't get his 15 cents worth.

MARY: What's that?

JACOB: First off, he lights up a cigarette, if he happens to have a tailor-made. That's number one: a Sweet Caporal.

MARY: What's number two?

JACOB: Number two is he cocks his feet on the seat of the fellow ahead, and if the fellow looks back, you stares at him like Tom Mix in "The

Lucky Horseshoe." A smirky sort of look that makes him slink low in his seat... Be quiet now. The picture's just begun ... Look, there's Tom now, riding up the road on his horse named Tony. That's some wonderful black horse, boy. See how his mane is permed and his tail all combed. And look how smart Tom looks in his same old get-up: silver spurs on the heels of his boots, that leather fit-out over his pants they calls chaps, that hanky knotted around his neck, and that tall hat with the wide brim and the crown stove in on both sides. See how straight Tom sits in the saddle, Mary. You'd swear he had an oar up his arse ...

MARY: I don't like language like that, Jacob! So just stop it!

JACOB: Sorry, maid. It just slipped out.

MARY: Besides, you said there was t'ree t'ings a fellow did in a picture show. You never mentioned the last.

JACOB: I was getting to that. Saving the best for later ... Now there always comes a time in the picture show, Mary, when the fella you'm with gets the sense ... the sense that the time is right.

MARY: The time for what?

JACOB: Well, say it's me, now. I'd glance out of the corner of my eye and see you sitting there with your hair all washed, your hands folded in your lap, looking all soft and lovely and smelling as fresh as the wind, and I'd sort of lean back in my seat like this and slip my arm around you ...

(JACOB does. MARY knocks his arm away and springs to her feet)

MARY: *(Indignantly)* So this is what you've been doing, is it, in the picture house with Rose?

JACOB: There is no Rose.

MARY: I don't believe you!

JACOB: I made her up.

MARY: Liar!

JACOB: Look, will you sit down and watch the picture? This is one of the best Tom ever made. He rides right into a wedding chapel and snatches the bride from under the nose of the groom.

(He grins)

STILL STANDS THE HOUSE

Gwen Pharis Ringwood

Place: a farmhouse, Saskatchewan prairie
Time: night, winter, 1930s
Characters: Hester, Ruth, Bruce

As a blizzard rages outside, Ruth and her sister-in-law Hester argue over the future of the Warren farm. Ruth has recently married into the Warren family. She cannot tolerate the isolation of the farm, and she dreads a similar fate for her soon-to-be-born child. She wants a place closer to town and has been urging her husband Bruce to strike a deal with Manning, the local real estate agent.

Hester is fanatical in her desire to stay in this house, on this parcel of land. It had been homesteaded by her (and Bruce's) father, whose portrait still graces the living room wall. Hester will go to great lengths in order to stay; at the end of the play, she will knowingly send her brother and his wife to their deaths. (Early in the play, Hester warns Ruth to fill the lantern with kerosene. But Ruth forgets and when, at the end of the scene below, Bruce leaves to fetch the mare, he takes along a lantern that will soon go out, leaving him stranded in the storm. Ruth later discovers her mistake and ventures out to look for him.)

Bruce Warren is caught between the two women. He echoes his sister's devotion to their father's memory, but also recognizes that the farm has not been financially viable. The basic antagonism in the play proceeds from locale and situation—three people versus a barren land in an untoward climate.

The scene begins after Ruth reveals her plans to redecorate the house with new curtains and a matching cover for "Father's chair." Hester is, of course, appalled.

HESTER: *(Throwing the chintz down)* This is Father's chair. I won't have it changed.

RUTH: I'm sorry, Hester. *(With spirit)* Must we keep everything the same forever?

HESTER: There's nothing in this house that isn't good, that wasn't bought with care and pride by one of us who loved it. This stuff is cheap and gaudy.

RUTH: It isn't dull and falling apart with age.

HESTER: Before my father died, when he was ill, he sat here in this chair where he could see them threshing from the window. It was the first time since he came here that he'd not been in the fields at harvest. Now you come - you who never knew him , who never saw him - and you won't rest until -

RUTH: Hester!

HESTER: You've got no right to touch it!

(Her hands grip the back of the old chair as she stands rigid, her eyes blazing. BRUCE Warren enters from outside, carrying a pail of milk. He is tall and dark, about 30 years old, sensitive and bitter. His vain struggle to make the farm pay since his father's death has left him with an oppressive sense of failure. He is proud and quick to resent an imagined reproach. He has dark hair, his shoulders are a little stooped, and he moves restlessly and abruptly. Despite his moodiness, he is extremely likable. He is dressed warmly in dark trousers, a sweater under his heavy leather coat, he wears gloves, cap, and high boots. He brushes the snow from his coat as he enters)

BRUCE: *(Carrying the milk into the kitchen)* Is the separator up, Ruth?

RUTH: Yes, it's all ready, Bruce. Wait, I'll help you.

(She follows him into the kitchen. HESTER stands at the chair a moment after they have gone; her eyes fall on the plant on the table. Slowly she goes toward it, as if drawn by something she hated. She looks down at the lavender blooms for a moment. Then with a quick, angry gesture, she crushes one of the stalks. She turns away and is winding up her wool when BRUCE and RUTH return)

RUTH: You must be frozen.

BRUCE: *(Taking off his coat and gloves)* I'm cold, all right. God, it's a blizzard: 38 below, and a high wind.

(He throws his coat over a chair at the table)

RUTH: *(With pride)* Did you see the hyacinths? They've bloomed since yesterday.

BRUCE: *(Smiling)* Yes, they're pretty. *(Touching them, he notices the broken stalk)* Looks like one of them's broken.

RUTH: Where? *(She sees it)* Oh, it is! And that one hadn't bloomed yet! I wonder ... It wasn't broken when I - *(RUTH turns accusingly to HESTER)* Hester!

(HESTER returns RUTH's look calmly)

HESTER: *(Coldly)* Yes?

RUTH: Hester, did you ...

BRUCE: *(Going over to the fire)* Oh, Ruth, don't make such a fuss about it. It can't be helped.

HESTER: I'll take care of the milk.

(She takes the small lamp from the window)

RUTH: I'll do it.

HESTER: *(Moving toward the kitchen)* You turn the separator so slow the cream's as thin as water.

RUTH: *(Stung to reply)* That's not true. You never give me a chance to -

BRUCE: *(Irritably)* For God's sake don't quarrel about it.

(He sits in the chair by the stove)

HESTER: I don't intend to quarrel. *(She goes into the kitchen. RUTH follows HESTER to the door. The sound of the separator comes from the kitchen. RUTH turns wearily, takes up the pot of hyacinths, and places them on the stand near the stove. Then sits on the footstool)*

RUTH: It's always that way.

BRUCE: *(Gazing moodily at the stove)* Why don't you two try to get along?

(A silence)

RUTH: Did you put the stock in?

(The question is merely something to fill the empty space of silence between them)

BRUCE: Yes. That black mare may foal tonight. I'll have to look at her later on.

RUTH: It's bitter weather for a little colt to be born.

BRUCE: Yes.

(Another silence. Finally RUTH, to throw off the tension between them, gets up and moves her footstool over to his chair)

RUTH: I'm glad you're here. I've been lonesome for you.

BRUCE: *(Putting his hand on hers)* I'm glad to be here.

RUTH: I thought of you out at the barn, trying to work in this cold.

BRUCE: I was all right. I'd hate to walk far tonight, though. You can't see your hand before your face.

RUTH: *(After a look at the kitchen)* Hester's been so strange again these last few days, Bruce.

BRUCE: I know it's hard, Ruth.

RUTH: It's like it was when I first came here. At everything I touch, she cries out like I'd hurt her somehow.

BRUCE: Hester has to do things her own way. She's always been like that.

RUTH: If only she could like me a little. I think she almost does sometimes, but then -

BRUCE: You think too much about her.

RUTH: Maybe it's because we've been shut in so close. I'm almost afraid of her lately.

BRUCE: She's not had an easy life, Ruth.

RUTH: I know that. She's talked about your father almost constantly today.

BRUCE: His death hit us both hard. Dad ran the farm, decided everything.

RUTH: It's been six years, Bruce.

BRUCE: There are things you don't count out by years.

RUTH: He wouldn't want you to go on remembering forever.

BRUCE: *(Looking at the floor)* No.

RUTH: You should get free of this house. It's not good for you stay here. It's not good for Hester. *(Getting up, she crosses to the sideboard and returns with the deed of sale, which she hands to BRUCE)* Mr. Manning left this for you. He's coming back tomorrow for it, when you've signed it.

(He takes the papers)

BRUCE: *(Annoyed by her assurance)* He doesn't need to get so excited. I haven't decided to sign it yet. He said he wouldn't need to know 'til spring.

(He goes over to the lamps at the table and studies the document)

RUTH: His company gave him orders to close the deal this week or let it go.

BRUCE: This week?

RUTH: That's what he said.

BRUCE: Well, I'll think about it.

RUTH: You'll have to decide tonight, Bruce. No one else will offer you as much. Five thousand dollars and an irrigated farm a mile from town seems a good price.

BRUCE: I'm not complaining about the deal. It's fair.

RUTH: *(Urgently)* You're going to take it, aren't you, Bruce?

BRUCE: I don't know. God, I don't know. *(He throws the document on the table)* I don't want to sell, Ruth. I think I'll try it another year.

RUTH: Bruce, you've struggled here too long now. You haven't had a crop, a good crop in five years.

BRUCE: I need to be told that.

RUTH: It's not your fault. But you've told me you ought to give it up, that it's too dry here.

BRUCE: We may get a crop this year. We're due for one.

RUTH: If you take this offer, we'll be nearer town. We'll have water on the place. We can have a garden, and trees growing.

BRUCE: That's about what those irrigated farms are - gardens.

RUTH: And Bruce, it wouldn't be so lonely there, so cruelly lonely.

BRUCE: I told you how it was before you came.

RUTH: *(Resenting his tone)* You didn't tell me you worshipped a house. That you made a god of a house and a section of land. You didn't tell me that!

BRUCE: *(Angrily)* You didn't tell me that you'd moon at a window for your old friends, either.
(He stands up and throws the deed of sale on the table)

RUTH: How could I help it here?

BRUCE: And you didn't tell me you'd be afraid of having a child. What kind of a woman are you that you don't want your child?

RUTH: That's not true.

BRUCE: No? You cried when you knew, didn't you?

RUTH: Bruce!

BRUCE: *(Going blindly on)* What makes you feel the way you do then? Other women have children without so much fuss. Other women are glad.

RUTH: *(Intensely angry)* Don't speak to me like that. Keep your land. Eat and sleep and dream land, I don't care!

BRUCE: *(Turning to the portrait of his father)* My father came out here and took a homestead. He broke the prairie with one plow and a team of horses. He built a house to live in out of the sod. You didn't know that, did you? He and Mother lived here in a sod shanty and struggled to make things grow. Then they built a one-roomed shack; and when the good years came, they built this house. The finest in the country! I thought my son would have it.

RUTH: *(Moving to him)* What is there left to give a son? A house that stirs with ghosts! A piece of wornout land where the rain never comes.

BRUCE: That's not all. I don't suppose you can understand.

RUTH: *(Turning away from him, deeply hurt)* No. I don't suppose I can. You give me little chance to know how you feel about things.

BRUCE: *(His anger gone)* Ruth, I didn't mean that. But you've always lived in town. *(He goes to the window and stands looking out for a moment, then turns)* Those rocks along the fence out there, I picked up every one of them with my own hands and carried them there. I've plowed that southern slope along the coulee every year since I was 12. *(His voice is torn with a kind of shame for his emotion.)* I feel about the land like Hester does about the house, I guess. I don't want to leave it. I don't want to give it up.

RUTH: *(Gently)* But it's poor land, Bruce.
(BRUCE sits down, gazing gloomily at the fire. HESTER comes in from the kitchen with the small lamp and places it on the sideboard. Then she sits at the table, taking up her knitting. As BRUCE speaks, she watches him intently)

BRUCE: Yes, it's strange that in a soil that won't grow trees a man can put roots down, but he can.

RUTH: *(At his side)* You'd feel the same about another place after a little while.

BRUCE: I don't know. When I saw the wind last spring blowing the dirt away, the dirt I'd plowed and harrowed and sowed to grain, I felt as though a part of myself was blowing away in the dust. Even now with the land three feet under snow I can look out and feel it waiting for the seed I've saved for it.

RUTH: But if we go, we'll be nearer other people, not cut off from everything that lives.

BRUCE: You need people, don't you?

HESTER: Yes. She needs them. I've seen her at the window, looking toward the town. Day after day she stands there.

(BRUCE and RUTH, absorbed in the conflict between them, had forgotten HESTER's presence. At HESTER's words, RUTH turns on them both, flaming with anger)

RUTH: You two. You're so PERFECT!

HESTER: *(Knitting)* We could always stand alone, the three of us. We didn't need to turn to every stranger who held his hand out.

RUTH: No! You'd sit here in this husk of a house, living like shadows, until these four walls closed in on you, buried you.

HESTER: I never stood at a window, looking down the road that leads to town.

RUTH: *(The pent-up hysteria of the day and the longing of months breaks through, tumbling out in her words)* It's not for myself I look down that road, Hester. It's for the child I'm going to have. You're right, Bruce. I am afraid. It's not what you think though, not for myself. You two and your father lived so long in this dark house that you forgot there's a world beating outside, forgot that people laugh and play sometimes. And you've shut me out! *(There is a catch in her voice)* I never would have trampled on your thoughts if you'd given them to me. But as it is, I might as well not be a person. You'd like a shadow better that wouldn't touch your house. A child would die here. A child can't live with shadows.

(Much disturbed, BRUCE rises and goes to her)

BRUCE: Ruth! I didn't know you hated it so much.

RUTH: I thought it would change. I thought I could change it. You know now.

BRUCE: *(Quietly)* Yes.

RUTH: *(Pleading)* If we go, I'll WANT this child, Bruce. don't you see? But I'm not happy here. What kind of a life will our child have? He'll be old before he's out of school. (She looks at the hyacinth on the stand)) He'll be like this hyacinth bud that's broken before it bloomed.

(BRUCE goes to the table and stands looking down at the deed of sale. His voice is tired and flat, but resolved)

BRUCE: All right. I'll tell Manning I'll let him have the place.

HESTER: *(Turning quickly to BRUCE)* What do you mean?

BRUCE: I'm going to sell the farm to Manning. He was here today.

HESTER: *(Standing up, her eyes blazing)* You can't sell this house.

BRUCE: *(Looking at the deed of sale)* Oh, Ruth's right. We can't make a living on the place. *(He sits down, leafing through the document)* It's too dry. And too far from the school.

HESTER: It wasn't too far for you to go, or me.

BRUCE: *(Irritably)* Do you think I want to sell?

HESTER: SHE does. But she can't do it. *(Her voice is low)* This house belongs to me.

BRUCE: Hester, don't start that again! I wish to God the land had been divided differently, but it wasn't.

HESTER: Father meant for us to stay here and keep things as they were when he was with us.

BRUCE: The soil wasn't blowing away when he was farming it.

HESTER: He meant for me to have the house.

RUTH: You'll go with us where we go, Hester.

HESTER: *(To RUTH)* You came here. You plotted with him to take this house from me. But it's mine!

BRUCE: *(His voice cracks through the room)* Stop that, Hester! I love this place as much as you do, but I'm selling it, I tell you. *(As he speaks, he gets up abruptly and, taking up his coat, puts it on. HESTER sinks slowly into the chair, staring. RUTH tries to put her hand on BRUCE's arm)*

RUTH: Bruce! Not that way! Not for me. If it's that way, I don't care enough.

BRUCE: *(Shaking himself free)* Oh, leave me alone!

RUTH: Bruce!

BRUCE: *(Going to the door)* I'll be glad when it's over, I suppose.

RUTH: Where are you going?

BRUCE: *(Taking his cap and gloves)* To look at that mare.

RUTH: Bruce! *(But he has gone)*

HESTER: *(Getting up, she goes to her father's chair and stands behind it, facing RUTH; she moves and speaks as if she were in a dream)* This is my house. I won't have strangers in it.

RUTH: *(At the table, without looking at HESTER)* Oh, Hester! I didn't want it to be this way. I tried -

HESTER: *(As if she were speaking to a stranger)* Why did you come here?

RUTH: I've hurt you. But I'm right about this. I know I'm right.

HESTER: There isn't any room for you.

RUTH: Can't you see? It's for all of us.

(HESTER comes toward RUTH with a strange, blazing anger in her face)

HESTER: I know your kind. In the night you tempted him with your bright hair.

RUTH: Hester!

HESTER: Your body anointed with jasmine for his pleasure.

RUTH: Hester, don't say such things.

HESTER: Oh, I know what you are! You and women like you. You put a dream around him with your arms, a sinful dream.

RUTH: *(Drawing back)* Hester!

HESTER: You lift your white face to every stranger like you offered him a cup to drink from. That's sin! That's lust after the forbidden fruit. *(Turning from RUTH, as if she had forgotten her presence, HESTER looks fondly at the room)* I'll never leave this house.

(BRUCE opens the door and comes in quickly and stormily. He goes into the kitchen as he speaks)

BRUCE: The mare's got out. She jumped the corral. I'll have to go after her.

RUTH: *(Concerned)* Bruce, where will she be?

BRUCE: *(Returning with an old blanket)* She'll be in the snowshed by the coulee. She always goes there when she's about to foal.

(HESTER sits in the chair by the stove, her knitting in her hand. She pays no attention to the others)

RUTH: But you can't go after her in this storm.

BRUCE: I'll take this old blanket to cover the colt, if it's born yet. Where's the lantern?

(He sees the two lanterns by the kitchen door, and taking one of them to the table lights it)

RUTH: It's three miles, Bruce. You mustn't go on foot. It's dangerous.

BRUCE: I'll have to. She'd never live through the night, or the colt either. *(He turns to go)* You'd better go to bed. Good night, Hester.

RUTH: Let me come with you.

BRUCE: No. *(Then as he looks at her, all resentment leaves him. He puts down the lantern, goes to her, and takes her in his arms)* Ruth, forget what I said. You know I didn't mean -

RUTH: *(Softly)* I said things I didn't mean, too -

BRUCE: I love you Ruth. You know it, don't you?

RUTH: Bruce!

(He kisses her, and for a moment their love is a flame in the room)

BRUCE: Don't worry. I won't be long.

RUTH: I'll wait.

(BRUCE goes out)

THEATRE OF THE FILM NOIR

George F. Walker

Place: Lilliane's apartment, Paris
Time: 1944
Characters: Inspector Clair, a police detective; Lilliane, a former shop
  girl

Lilliane's brother Jean was murdered in a back street, even as the allied
  forces marched into Paris. Who murdered him? His lover Bernard,
  who now wants a "marriage of convenience" with Lilliane? Or
  Lilliane's lover Eric, a German soldier who also happens to have slept
  with Jean? At any rate, Lilliane has much to hide - whether it be her
  Nazi lover or her acquaintance with the French Communist Party.

LILLIANE's apartment. LILLIANE is sitting. INSPECTOR Clair is standing.
INSPECTOR: You don't mind if I ask you a few questions?
LILLIANE: No. But I've already told several other policemen every-
  thing I know.
INSPECTOR: Of course. But this is such an unusual case ... I'm sorry
  I didn't notice, you have your coat on. Were you on your way out?
  I mean, you did get the message that I was coming.
LILLIANE: Actually I just got in.
INSPECTOR: Really. I must have missed you.
LILLIANE: What was that.
INSPECTOR: On my way into your building I met an old friend. He
  kept me in conversation for almost an hour.
LILLIANE: I came in the back way.
INSPECTOR: Of course. You have a back entrance. That must have
  been very helpful over the past little while.
LILLIANE: What do you mean?

INSPECTOR: Well, the war, the occupation made everyone so tense. So suspicious. It was difficult for an attractive young person ... to go about her business.

LILLIANE: I've never paid any attention to other people's opinions of me.

INSPECTOR: Good for you. And you have no political activity.

LILLIANE: No. Unless you consider the business of survival a political activity.

INSPECTOR: Under the circumstances, perhaps.

LILLIANE: It would be easy to say I was in the resistance. So many people are saying that now, I know. But I was scared. Scared of starvation.

INSPECTOR: Well no matter what we did or did not do for whatever reason, I suppose we must all begin again somehow.

LILLIANE: If we can.

INSPECTOR: Yes. Which unfortunately brings us back to your brother's death.

LILLIANE: The Communists killed him.

INSPECTOR: So you said in your statement. Because they suspected he was a spy, is that right.

LILLIANE: Yes.

INSPECTOR: But you didn't say why they suspected that.

LILLIANE: Because I didn't know. Jean didn't tell me.

INSPECTOR: He just told you that he was suspected.

LILLIANE: He said they were giving him a rough time. He was afraid of them.

INSPECTOR: That's all he told you. What I'm saying is, did he actually tell you they suspected him of spying on them.

LILLIANE: That's what they fear most. That's what they always assume. I know how they are.

INSPECTOR: You've had personal experience with them.

LILLIANE: I have friends who were with Communists.

INSPECTOR: You do?

LILLIANE: Friends of friends. I gave the names already.

INSPECTOR: Yes. None of them were helpful. By the time we reached them none of them were even Communists. Affiliations change so rapidly these days. One of these former Communists was also a known collaborator with the Nazis. He is now very friendly with the Americans. Ah well. I suppose he too is just trying to survive.

LILLIANE: I survived without affiliations.

INSPECTOR: Good for you. On the night Jean was killed, he visited here. Correct?

LILLIANE: We had dinner. We talked.

INSPECTOR: Yes. Your apartment is so cozy. So safe. It was a nice relaxing evening?

LILLIANE: He was tense. He was going to that rally.

INSPECTOR: He expected trouble.

LILLIANE: There was always trouble. The Communists attracted it like flies.

INSPECTOR: But this time Jean wouldn't know which side his trouble would be coming from. Did he go to the meeting alone.

LILLIANE: Someone picked him up.

INSPECTOR: Who.

LILLIANE: I don't know. There was a knock on the door. Jean answered it. Grabbed his coat and left. I didn't see who it was.

INSPECTOR: None of this was in your statement.

LILLIANE: None of these questions were asked.

INSPECTOR: Of course. Well even the police department is in the process of rebuilding.

LILLIANE: But you are not new at this.

INSPECTOR: Oh no. No I'm not new. I still make mistakes, though. Is that chocolate in your pocket.

LILLIANE: Yes. Would you like a piece.

INSPECTOR: Please.

(She hands it to him. He breaks off a piece)

American chocolate.

LILLIANE: English.

INSPECTOR: I thought only American soldiers had this.

LILLIANE: English chocolate, Inspector. From a Free French soldier. They give it out freely. They give it to anyone. They give it to old women, young men, children. They just laugh and give it to you for no reason.

INSPECTOR: Good for them. Well. The problem is, we've talked to the Communists. They say they liked Jean. They say he had just been elected to a responsible position in the party. Their position does not make things easy.

LILLIANE: They're lying.

INSPECTOR: Perhaps. But they lie so well. In any event, it does not make things easy.

LILLIANE: Did you expect they would be.

INSPECTOR: No. *(Hands her the rest of the chocolate)* Can I visit you again. I might have more questions.

LILLIANE: Any time.

(She offers the chocolate to him. He smiles. Takes it)

INSPECTOR: Thank you. In the meantime good luck. What are your plans.

LILLIANE: I'm not going anywhere.

INSPECTOR: I meant for work.

LILLIANE: I have a friend who knows an American soldier who makes films. I would like to be an actress.

INSPECTOR: Be careful of that kind of American film.

LILLIANE: I love American films.

INSPECTOR: Yes, but ... Never mind. You would be very good in films, I'm sure. I hope you get the chance.

LILLIANE: I will. I've made my mind up.

INSPECTOR: I'll show myself out.

LILLIANE: Be careful. The stairway is very dark.

INSPECTOR: In that case, perhaps I should let myself out the back.

LILLIANE: No.

   (Blackout)

TIT-COQ

Gratien Gélinas

Place: a reading room in a military hospital in England
Time: December, 1944
Characters: Tit-Coq, Jean-Paul

Tit-Coq and Jean-Paul, both in the Canadian army, got into a fight over
a girl in 1942. Jean-Paul called Tit-Coq a "damn little bastard," which
would not have been upsetting except that it was true. Tit-Coq was
an orphan, raised by nuns and given the name Arthur St. Jean (he's
called Tit-Coq, presumably, because he's easily provoked).

Their Commanding Officer punished the two soldiers by requiring
them to spend Christmas together in St. Anicet with Jean-Paul's
family. Tit-Coq and Jean-Paul agreed—and that is how Tit-Coq
became acquainted with Jean-Paul's sister Marie-Ange.

Marie-Ange has promised to wait for Tit-Coq while he is fighting
overseas. But the wait has been long, and will be longer. Marie-Ange
corresponds faithfully. Still, Tit-Coq fears that she has reneged on
her vow.

JEAN-PAUL is seated at a table writing at TIT-COQ's dictation. The latter,
his right arm in a sling, turns his back to JEAN-PAUL.
TIT-COQ: Uh ... wait a minute. *(Dictating)* "As for my fracture, don't
worry. In three weeks ..."
JEAN-PAUL: Hey, not so quick! *(Writing)* "In three weeks ..."
TIT-COQ: "In three weeks, I'll be punching the bag ... uh ... punching
the bag." *(To JEAN-PAUL)* ... Read it back, to see if it's all right.
JEAN-PAUL: *(Reads back)* "As for my fracture -
TIT-COQ: *(Interrupting him)* No, from the start.
JEAN-PAUL: "Dear Marie-Ange, ... If the present letter seems to be
written with a foot, it's no fault of mine, seeing Jean-Paul is writing
it for me ..." *(To TIT-COQ)* Think how good I was, suggesting myself
to start like that.
TIT-COQ: Keep going! Don't stop!
JEAN-PAUL: *(Reading)* " ... Because I've had my right arm in a sling for
three weeks, through a damn silly fracture in maneuvers." *(To TIT-*

COQ) ... "Damn." You're sure you want me to write that?

TIT-COQ: Yes, yes ... A damn silly fracture, that's what it is.

JEAN-PAUL: *(Continuing)* " ... In maneuvers. I fell flat on my face jumping from a truck. I don't expect I'll get the Victoria Cross for that!"

TIT-COQ: *(Stops him, surprised)* Where did that come from?

JEAN-PAUL: Well, I put it in myself, yes. If you find it corny, maybe she'll laugh at it.

TIT-COQ: *(Curtly)* This is no time to write nonsense!

JEAN-PAUL: *(Changing tone)* If you're in too good a humor, I can scram out of here. I'm using my afternoon off to come and write a love letter to my own sister.

TIT-COQ: Do as you please: I'm not holding you.

JEAN-PAUL: *(A moment, he considers TIT-COQ, whose back is turned, then)* Damn independent character! He's got his right arm in a cast, he's dying to be heard from, he's caught like a mouse in a trap, and yet he indulges in the luxury of kicking people in the ass. *(Conciliating)* Well, I'm not walking out. That letter's got to go! Three weeks you've been unable to write; if that keeps up, Marie-Ange is going to worry.

TIT-COQ: Worry? Maybe not so much.

JEAN-PAUL: Marie-Ange?

TIT-COQ: Yes!

JEAN-PAUL: Say, what's got into you? You didn't crack your brain too, when you fell, eh?

TIT-COQ: I'm not blind, that's all!

JEAN-PAUL: She's stopped calling you "My Precious Lovey-dovey"? Or she don't write so often?

TIT-COQ: She writes every week; only they read between the lines, her letters. She's sick or tired, or just slipping through my fingers, I don't know ... but there's something queer going on, I'm sure of that.

JEAN-PAUL: Come, come! My sister, she's a girl on the level. If she's promised to wait, she'll keep her word.

TIT-COQ: Exactly! Her word: that might be the only thing that keeps her!

JEAN-PAUL: You should never have broken that arm, you!

TIT-COQ: Oh, that's been buzzing around in my head for quite a while, *(Showing his sling)* long before this. I've even got in my pack a letter I composed last month. I haven't sent it yet, but I will, if this keeps up.

JEAN-PAUL: What sweet yarn do you spin in that letter?

TIT-COQ: This: if she feels like it, she's perfectly free to change her mind about waiting for me. It's love I want, not charity!

JEAN-PAUL: O.K. But think twice before mailing it, your *billet doux.* Sometimes, we want to play independent, so we open the door, to show the other one she can walk out if she feels like it. She stays, of course. Only, the open door makes a draft. She catches a stiff neck ... and suffers ... through our fault ... At worst, what's worrying you is a little tiff by remote control. These things happen even to lovers holding hands seven nights a week. All the more for you when you've been 3000 miles apart for 18 months.

TIT-COQ: Yes. Eighteen months we've been writing, damn it. At the beginning, each envelope came like Easter Sunday. To read: "Sealed with a kiss" gave you butterflies in the stomach. And just writing a dozen Xs under your name, in the answer, made you shake in the legs. But when you've been writing Xs for a year and a half, you finally realize it's always the same old platitudes that keep popping up, seeing that you left school at 14.

JEAN-PAUL: If it's new platitudes you're looking for, I can always try and dig a couple up for you.

TIT-COQ: Besides, those letters take a hundred years to get there. When your yearning spills over, you grab your pen to say so. But right away you realize she's going to read your lamentation in six weeks. And if she answers: "I'm yearning for you too!" you'll find out in three months!

JEAN-PAUL: *(Who wants to make TIT-COQ laugh at any rate)* It reminds me of the two closed-mouth fellows that lived together. One fine day, one of them makes a move to speak and says to the other ...

TIT-COQ: *(Pursuing his idea)* If I could only talk to her two minutes, face to face! I'd wind her up again for a year, and I'd get my own balance back in the bargain. But no! Always nothing but this damn paper. *(With his left fist he bangs the armchair)*

JEAN-PAUL: Hey! Watch out you don't bust the other arm, you.

TIT-COQ: If you're trying to make me laugh with your stupid jokes, you're wasting your time.

JEAN-PAUL: Well, there you are! We've all got our own way of cheering up friends. If you like the other way better, we can lie down on the floor and bawl for a couple of hours! Only I'd be surprised if we ended up better off. *(Serious)* Listen, Tit-Coq, I see you in the dumps over nothing; I want to buck you up, so I poke fun at everything, like my dad. Maybe I'm no funnier than my mom, but at bottom I'm pulling for you hundred percent! Here, I'm going to tell you a mushy one: you're my brother more than anybody else. And I'd be happy as hell for you if, some fine morning, I could be your best man, down the center aisle, with a rose in my buttonhole and a brand-new haircut.

TIT-COQ: You sure of that?

JEAN-PAUL: Why, of course! And everyone feels like me in the family.

TIT-COQ: Yes, eh? Because, after all, that's what I'm scared of: they might gang up on me over there.

JEAN-PAUL: Well, I'd like to see just one of them at it!

TIT-COQ: What about that guy Vermette? Do you think he's still hanging around her, like he used to?

JEAN-PAUL: He hasn't got a chance! Why don't you stop fretting? You busted your arm in a stupid way: it gets on your nerves, so you see everything black, that's all. Besides, you know you'll change units, because of that accident. You and I will take different trails, and so you won't be able to bawl me out for a while.

TIT-COQ: *(Upset)* You think ... I'm going to be transferred, yes?

JEAN-PAUL: Why, sure! Depend on that! But don't complain; while we cross the Channel and take it on the chin, you have the chance to end up as a barman in some mess.

TIT-COQ: To hell with that chance.

JEAN-PAUL: Now, while we're waiting for that blessed day, we've got to get this letter written. And I must be back to camp by five o'clock: I have some orders to give to the general. *(Rereading)* "As for my fracture, don't worry. In three weeks I'll be punching the bag." *(He writes)* "What bothers me most, I cannot wave my right arm when I am speaking ..."

(Curtain)

TIT-COQ

Gratien Gélinas

Place: outside Germaine's door, Montreal
Time: September 1945
Characters: Tit-Coq, Germaine

Tit-Coq returns from the war to find that Marie-Ange has married
Leopold Vermette, a young man from a wealthy family. Wishing to
see Marie-Ange one last time, Tit-Coq shows up at the apartment she
once shared with her cousin Germaine.

Germaine has never been sympathetic toward Tit-Coq. She regards him
as a no-account "little soldier coming from God knows where and
who's liable to go away any day." She has given her blessing,
meanwhile, to Marie-Ange's union with Leopold Vermette. The
antagonism between Germaine and Tit-Coq is evident in the following scene.

GERMAINE, *coming from left, goes toward the door. As she is about to put
the key into the lock, TIT-COQ emerges from the shadow, right.*
TIT-COQ: Hello, Germaine!
GERMAINE: *(Starts)* My God, you scared me! ... Good evening, Tit-
Coq.
TIT-COQ: I rang just now ... There was no answer, so I decided to wait.
GERMAINE: *(Ill at ease)* That's right.
TIT-COQ: Then, you're still living here.
GERMAINE: Yes, I kept the apartment for myself when - *(She hesitates)*
TIT-COQ: - Marie-Ange got married, Marie-Ange got married! Say it.
Why be bashful? It's quite simple!
GERMAINE: *(In a voice she means to be serene)* What can I do for you?
TIT-COQ: Can't you make a little guess?
GERMAINE: *(Artless)* No ...
TIT-COQ: Jean-Paul was lucky enough to land a day before me; so he
must have told you of my plans in a flash.
GERMAINE: Why, no ...
TIT-COQ: *(Incredulous)* You don't say!
GERMAINE: Honest to God.
TIT-COQ: All right, if you insist on playing innocent to the end, I'll

have to say it in black and white: I want to see her again.

GERMAINE: Poor you, she's married. What is it going to give you?

TIT-COQ: Take it easy: I don't plan to cling around her neck. Only I've decided to spin her a piece of my mind, before scramming out of this town.

GERMAINE: That's a poor consolation.

TIT-COQ: Times are tough. I grab what I can.

GERMAINE: *(Looking for an escape)* She won't be able to come, because she's away ... on a trip.

TIT-COQ: *(Quickly)* Where?

GERMAINE: Uh ... Well ...

TIT-COQ: Well, you lie! I'm terribly sorry, but you lie. You weren't quick enough with that one. What's more I'll read your cards and inform you that you've been spending the evening together ... wondering what mug you'd make if ever I came back in the picture. No! You know damn well she's in town. She leaving her dear little husband like that? Never!

GERMAINE: *(Well-meaning)* As a matter of fact, her husband's away.

TIT-COQ: Don't tell me they've already stopped sleeping on the same pillow?

GERMAINE: No, but he was drafted for the army two months ago.

TIT-COQ: Well, bless my soul if that ain't too bad! So he's in the army too? Where did they ship him?

GERMAINE: He's stationed somewhere in Ontario.

TIT-COQ: Poor boy, it must have been quite a job, prying him out of bed, eh? *(Jeers)* Yes, that's a damn good one! God is more just than we think, after all. *(Bitter)* I hope she's kept copies of the love letters she sent me. It must make it easier to write and say she adores him.

GERMAINE: To come back to Marie-Ange -

TIT-COQ: *(Cutting her short)* To come back to Marie-Ange, whether she's away or not, you're going to tell the lady I want to see her.

GERMAINE: I can say right now that she won't meet you.

TIT-COQ: All right, then! *(Producing a paper from his pocket, he reads)* "Mrs. Leopold Vermette, 3417 Fullum Street." *(To GERMAINE)* That's her correct address isn't it? What's more, if my tip is on the level, that's where the in-laws live too? If she insists on my making a little scene in their parlor, I don't mind going all the way.

GERMAINE: There's a police, you know, for those tricks.

TIT-COQ: Why, sure, go right ahead. It would make a hell of a nice trial. If the intimacy of the young couple can gain anything from it, I'm in favor one hundred percent. *(Anger raises his voice)* Because you seem to forget I have nothing to lose in all that.

GERMAINE: Not so loud! What will the neighbors say?

TIT-COQ: *(Bursting out)* I don't give a damn for the neighbors! Matter of fact, I don't give a damn for anybody.

GERMAINE: *(Who is losing countenance more and more)* Where would you want to see her?

TIT-COQ: Upstairs, here. We've already been so happy up there, why make any change?

GERMAINE: *(Giving in)* Anyhow, I'll give her your message.

TIT-COQ: That's right. Here, tomorrow night, eight o'clock. And I warn you, let Jean-Paul keep his nose out of this, or there'll be some window smashing. As for you, I suggest you go and take the air in the corridor. Because it's my hunch she'd rather be alone to hear me - question of pride you know. Besides it will soon be over. Five minutes at most! The time you need to pull a rotten tooth. A tooth that can go on nagging a long time if you neglect it ... and form an abscess. You get me?

GERMAINE: Yes, I get you.

TIT-COQ: Then I've got no more to say. Good night! *(He turns on his heel and goes out)*

WAITING FOR THE PARADE

John Murrell

Place: Calgary, Alberta
Time: early 1940s
Characters: Catherine, in her early 30s; Eve, in her 20s

Waiting For The Parade is a play about five women and how they manage to survive the war years. Two of those women, Catherine and Eve, throw themselves with gusto into the new fashions; here they are experimenting with hairstyles.

Catherine's husband Billy was among the first Calgarians to enlist when the Second World War broke out. She admires him for his sense of honor but still has unresolved feelings about his enlistment: "there ought to be some space for good sense and—a little mutual respect," she says. She will later have an affair with Jim, a colleague in the munitions factory where she works.

Eve, on the other hand, is married to a man far older than she— too old, in fact, to be eligible for the army. She is horrified by the brutality of the war and by her inability to alleviate any of the suffering it causes.

CATHERINE *is standing in front of EVE, with her back to the audience, brushing EVE's hair. Both wear large towels around their shoulders.*
CATHERINE: Stop wiggling! Wait a second. There. Now you're gorgeous.
(She steps away from EVE. Both have put "fashionable" white streaks through their hair)
CATHERINE: Now you're perfection.
(She gives EVE a hand mirror. EVE looks at herself)
EVE: Oh no. Harry will kill me.
CATHERINE: I like it.
EVE: If HE doesn't kill me, the superintendent of schools will. *(She lowers the mirror)* What do you really think?

CATHERINE: I think we're both gorgeous.

EVE: *(Looking in the mirror again)* I look like a cross between Rita Hayworth and a skunk.

(CATHERINE laughs and tries to take the mirror from her)

CATHERINE: You'll get used to it.

(EVE hangs on to the mirror)

EVE: Harry will kill me.

CATHERINE: Put the mirror down.

EVE: *(Still looking in the mirror)* It just isn't the proper image for an educator. You don't know. Those Grade 10s can be vicious.

CATHERINE: Put the mirror down! Give yourself a minute to adjust.

EVE: Harry will kill me.

CATHERINE: For God's sake, put the mirror down!

(She reaches for the mirror. EVE quickly puts it down in her lap)

CATHERINE: Let's talk about something else.

EVE: All right. *(Pause)* What?

CATHERINE: I got a letter yesterday.

(She takes the letter from her dress pocket)

EVE: So you said.

CATHERINE: The first one in weeks. It's his second winter over there - *(She reads from the letter)* "So cold and damp, the birds are dying of rheumatism in mid-air and dropping to the ground, dead on arrival."

EVE: Not seriously?

CATHERINE: Billy's afraid his regiment's gone sour on the war. *(She reads from the letter)* "Six months we've been sitting around in tents, not enough room to stand up in. We're ready as we'll ever be, but nobody's said a word about moving any Canadians to the front. Another month and we'll be soft again."

(Pause)

EVE: *(Starting to raise the mirror)* May I look at my hair now?

CATHERINE: Not yet.

EVE: *(Putting the mirror down)* Well, do we have to talk about the war? I get enough of that from Harry. It'll only depress us. Isn't anything else happening in the world anymore?

CATHERINE: *(Putting the letter away)* For instance?

(Pause)

EVE: I was looking at our enrollment for next year. Guess how many boys have registered for Grade 12 Matric. Guess.

CATHERINE: I give up.

EVE: Eight. EIGHT. And half of those will be sneaking off to the recruiting station before mid-term. While I'm drilling them in the socio-political history of Greece, they're daydreaming about machine guns. "The Bren - the mighty Bren!" they call it.

(She makes a loud noise, like a machine gun)

CATHERINE: Don't talk about the war. It'll only depress us.

EVE: Harry greets me with that insane noise at the breakfast table every morning. *(She makes the machine gun noise again)* Then he laughs his head off. He's never fully recovered from being told he's too old for active service. *(Pause)* I should've married someone nearer to my own age. Senility strikes early in Harry's family. *(Pause. Raising the mirror again)* May I look at my hair now?

CATHERINE: Not yet!

(She snatches the mirror, glances at her own hair, then lays the mirror aside)

EVE: Well, let's not talk about Harry anymore.

CATHERINE: I second that motion.

(Pause)

EVE: Tell me about your work, down at the plant?

CATHERINE: Not much to tell. I make sandwiches. I sell Orange Kik and jujubes four times a day. It's somewhere to go, something to do. And I need the money.

EVE: Working around all those men - it doesn't make you nervous?

CATHERINE: Men have never made me nervous.

EVE: They've never made me anything but. *(Pause)* May I look at -?

CATHERINE: NOT YET.

(Pause)

EVE: Last week Harry joined the Mounted Constabulary.

CATHERINE: The what?

EVE: The Calgary Mounted Constabulary! Ta-ta! A bunch of old men with horses and chaps and pith helmets. From dusk to dawn they bravely patrol the Reservoir. On guard against enemy infiltration! I asked Harry, "Who would want to infiltrate a reservoir?" I thought he was going to hit me. *(Pause)* Did you write Billy for permission to take a job?

CATHERINE: *(Laughs and shakes her head)* He would've said "no."

EVE: And if he finds out, he'll be angry?

CATHERINE: He'll be ashamed. He'll feel like he's let us down.

EVE: But you don't feel that way?

CATHERINE: I try not to think about it. "There's a war on."

EVE: *(Rising suddenly)* Please, please don't say that! I'm sick of hearing it! Listen, you know what the latest insanity is?

CATHERINE: Why don't you sit down?

EVE: *(Beginning to pace)* I read that Leslie Howard has offered his services to the British war effort! LESLIE HOWARD!

CATHERINE: Maybe you should look at your hair now.

EVE: I wanted to scream! And they're bombing Great Britain! GREAT BRITAIN!

CATHERINE: I know that. Billy's there.

EVE: They're bombing Great Britain! They're bombing France! They're bombing Norway! They're bombing Belgium! We're back in the Dark

Ages! Wasting lives, spilling blood all over Europe!

CATHERINE: Sit down!

EVE: *(Pacing more and more frantically)* And Leslie Howard's in the middle of all that! An actor! A distinguished artist! Your Billy can hardly wait for a chance to be a part of the slaughter! And my husband would be leading the dance of death with a saber if he weren't too old! But they said it'd all be over in a few months! I remember an editorial - in the Toronto paper -! Oh God!

(CATHERINE has risen, crosses to EVE, catches her by the shoulders and shakes her. Pause. EVE's head droops)

EVE: Sorry. The first thing they taught us at Normal School was self-control. An educator mustn't lose her grip on herself. Sorry.

CATHERINE: At least you forgot about your damned hair for a minute. *(Putting one arm around EVE's shoulders, she offers her the mirror)* Go ahead. Take a peek. And I'll buy you a Coca Cola if you don't feel one hundred percent better about it now.

(EVE takes the mirror, holds it close and looks at herself. She bursts into tears, drops the mirror and covers her face with both hands. CATHERINE holds her)

YOU'RE GONNA BE ALRIGHT, JAMIE BOY

David Freeman

Place: living room of the Dinsdale house
Time: unspecified; the play had its first printing in 1974
Characters: Fran Dinsdale, in her 50s; her son Jamie, about 21

Jamie Dinsdale has just been released from the Clarke Institute of
Psychiatry (in Toronto). He is living with his parents, at the moment,
and seeing an analyst regularly. His father Ernie cares deeply for
Jamie but maintains that his son should not "go discussing any of
our personal affairs" with a psychiatrist. Ernie is referring, perhaps,
to what he sees as a shameful episode in Jamie's recent past: while
away at university, Jamie befriended a young homosexual named
Lenny who, although Jamie did not recognize it, wanted to have sex
with him. Ernie, on one of his frequent trips to the campus, was
introduced to Lenny and reacted antagonistically—offering to buy
Lenny a dress and then threatening "to come down and beat the shit
out of him." Unsure about his feelings toward Lenny, Jamie had a
breakdown. "That, and other things," he says, landed him in the
Clarke Institute.

It is difficult, however, to pinpoint the source of Jamie's psychiatric
troubles. The "other things" he refers to are his family, who do not
seem to know how to get close to one another. Freeman's play is a
condemnation of current middle class values that have moved away
from solid familial relationships to weeknights spent without conversation in front of the television set.

Tonight is "Family Night," when the Dinsdales usually congregate and watch Mod Squad and Adam 12. Jamie's sister Carol and her "super-stud" husband Fred will be coming over, but they do not expect Jamie to be at home. In this scene from the beginning of the play,

JAMIE DINSDALE, a young man of about 21, is sitting watching television, very lethargic. Enter FRAN, his mother, a woman in her 50s, with two bowls of potato chips. She looks at JAMIE, a little annoyed, and sets the bowl down.

FRAN: Are you going to sit there all day? *(No response)* I could use some help, you know.

(Still no response. She gives an annoyed shrug and exits. In a few seconds she re-enters, carrying another bowl of chips)

Day in, day out, ever since you've come home. Nothing but sit and stare at that damn television. You keep that up, you'll wind up right back in the asylum.

(JAMIE reaches over to steal a chip. FRAN smacks his hand)

FRAN: Not before dinner.

JAMIE: Institute.

FRAN: What?

JAMIE: Clarke Institute of Psychiatry.

FRAN: Different name. Same kind of people.

JAMIE: Why so many potato chips?

FRAN: Your father complained there weren't enough last time.

JAMIE: Well, if certain parties didn't pick them up by the fistfuls every five minutes, there'd be enough. By the way, Superstud is coming tonight, isn't he?

FRAN: If by that you mean Fred, yes, he is.

JAMIE: I thought Wednesday was his bowling night.

FRAN: Not any more. He joined a new league over in the West End, and they bowl Fridays. *(Inspecting everything)* Oh, God.

JAMIE: What's wrong?

FRAN: I forgot the peanuts.

JAMIE: So?

FRAN: Your father likes peanuts.

JAMIE: He's also got the hots for Doris Day, Mom, but he's not getting her tonight either.

FRAN: Jamie, this is serious. He'll sulk and brood all night.

JAMIE: Yeah, and treat you like a slave. It'll be last night all over again.

FRAN: Jamie, what are we going to do?

JAMIE: No sweat. I'll run down and get some.

FRAN: You can't. The store's closed by now.

JAMIE: Then just tell him they were sold out.

FRAN: But what if he checks?

JAMIE: He won't check.

FRAN: He might. Remember last time when I forgot the beer?

JAMIE: Mom, you gotta admit it was pretty dumb telling him Brewers Retail was all sold out.

FRAN: Boy, was he mad. He didn't speak to me for a whole week.

JAMIE: Why don't you just tell him to shove it.

FRAN: Be a good boy, and get the beer out of the fridge.

JAMIE: Why? If I take it out now it'll get warm.

FRAN: Fred likes it warm. He says if it's too cold it loses flavor.

JAMIE: Fine. If Freddy-boy wants a warm beer he can haul his ass down to the basement and get one.

FRAN: Just get the beer. *(She switches off the TV)*

JAMIE: Alright, alright.

(He exits to the kitchen. FRAN starts to set up the TV trays)

JAMIE: *(Offstage)* Tell me, Mom, do you really enjoy it?

FRAN: Enjoy what?

JAMIE: Family night.

FRAN: Well, your father seems to like it.

JAMIE: *(Entering)* I'm not talking about Dad. I'm talking about you.

FRAN: Well sure, I enjoy it. Why not? We get to watch all those programs together. Besides, it's a chance to see Carol.

JAMIE: What kind of mood do you think she'll be in tonight? *(Silence)* She was really upset on the phone this morning, wasn't she?

FRAN: You should have let me tell her where you were, Jamie.

JAMIE: She doesn't need me on her mind, Mom. She's got enough problems of her own. *(Pause)* Enough beer?

FRAN: For now.

JAMIE: Mom, can we watch "Chariots of the Gods" tonight?

FRAN: What?

JAMIE: "Chariots of the Gods."

FRAN: What's that?

JAMIE: It's a documentary based on some guy's theory that the ancient gods were really astronauts.

FRAN: I thought you'd be past that stage by now.

JAMIE: What stage?

FRAN: You know, rockets, space monsters, stuff like that.

JAMIE: It's a very good documentary, Mom.

FRAN: Okay, what time is this thing on?

JAMIE: Seven o'clock.

FRAN: Seven o'clock! What about "Mod Squad"?

JAMIE: You see that every week.

FRAN: But Carol likes it. She likes that guy on it. Michael what's his name.

JAMIE: Mom, I'm not asking for much. I don't even like TV. I just want to watch this one thing.

FRAN: If it was any other night, I'd say okay, but this is family night, and -

JAMIE: Screw family night! I don't give a shit about family night!

FRAN: Now, Jamie, don't get upset!

JAMIE: I'm not upset. *(But he is)* Mom, just because I get angry, it doesn't mean I'm going off my rocker.

FRAN: I know that, dear. Look, we'll talk it over with your father when he gets home, okay? We'll let him decide. After all, it's his set.

JAMIE: It may be his set, but it was supposed to be my surprise.

FRAN: Surprise?

JAMIE: Yeah, every time he came to the Clarke he kept hinting there was something waiting for me at home. Some surprise.

ZASTROZZI

George F. Walker

Place: a secluded square in an unspecified Italian city
Time: the 1890s
Characters: Zastrozzi, Julia

Zastrozzi is the most famous master criminal of the 1890s. He is a suberb
fencer, with words and with swords. He possesses a mind so powerful
and so evil that his nightmares "could petrify the devil."

Zastrozzi has come to Italy to avenge the death of his mother. The
fugitive from Zastrozzi's wrath is a demented artist named Verezzi.
In an earlier scene, Verezzi has shown interest in the fair-haired,
aristocratic beauty Julia. She has dismissed Verezzi as a fool.

Zastrozzi is not interested in merely killing his victim. He enjoys the
chase; the search for an ingenious revenge has become his *raison
d'etre*. Indeed, the seduction of Julia may be a means of making that
search more interesting.

*Evening. A secluded place. ZASTROZZI is sitting inert. JULIA comes on with
a picnic basket.*
JULIA: Excuse me sir. But do you mind if I sit here?
*(ZASTROZZI slowly turns toward her. Looks at her impassively for a
moment)*
ZASTROZZI: It would be best if you did not.
JULIA: But I always come here at this time on this particular day of the
week to have my picnic.
ZASTROZZI: Without fail?
JULIA: Yes.
ZASTROZZI: Well today you have been broken of a very silly habit.
Move on.
JULIA: Why should I?
ZASTROZZI: I want to be alone.
JULIA: Then you move on.
ZASTROZZI: I want to be alone. And I want to be alone exactly where
I am.
JULIA: Well today you are not going to get what you want. I am sitting
and I am eating.
(She eats and ZASTROZZI watches her for a moment)

ZASTROZZI: You are an only child from a very wealthy family.

JULIA: Perhaps.

ZASTROZZI: You don't have a worry in the world.

JULIA: Perhaps not.

ZASTROZZI: You don't have a thought in your head.

JULIA: I have one or two.

ZASTROZZI: And you are a virgin? *(Pause)* Well, are you or are you not a virgin?

JULIA: Why? Are you looking for one?

ZASTROZZI: Go away.

JULIA: In good time. Perhaps when I'm finished eating this piece of cheese. Perhaps after I eat my apple. In good time.
(Pause)

ZASTROZZI: Do you know who I am?

JULIA: No. Who are you?

ZASTROZZI: I am the man who is going to take away your virginity.

JULIA: Many have tried. All have failed. It will never be taken away. It will be given. In good time.

ZASTROZZI: Yes. Before you eat your apple to be exact.

JULIA: I'll scream.

ZASTROZZI: If you scream it will be the last sound you ever hear.

JULIA: Then I'll go limp. You won't enjoy it.

ZASTROZZI: It's not important that I enjoy it. It's important that you enjoy it.

JULIA: Impossible.

ZASTROZZI: Look at me.

JULIA: No. I don't think I will.

ZASTROZZI: Why not? Don't you find me attractive?

JULIA: That's not the point. You've threatened to rape me.

ZASTROZZI: Surely you knew I was joking.

JULIA: You didn't sound like you were joking.

ZASTROZZI: I was only trying to hide the embarrassing truth.

JULIA: And what might that be?

ZASTROZZI: That like so many other men I have admired you from a distance and could never gather the courage to approach you.

JULIA: So you waited here knowing I was coming on this particular day?

ZASTROZZI: Yes.

JULIA: And you adopted an aggressive attitude to disguise your true and romantic feelings for me.

ZASTROZZI: Yes.

JULIA: Yes. I can believe that. Men have done sillier things for me. Do you still want me to look at you?

ZASTROZZI: No. I'm too embarrassed.

JULIA: I understand.

ZASTROZZI: Just look ahead.

JULIA: If you wish.
(Pause)
ZASTROZZI: I hope you don't mind that I'm doing this?
JULIA: What?
ZASTROZZI: Running my hand through your hair.
(He does nothing. He will do nothing)
JULIA: Oh. I don't feel anything.
ZASTROZZI: I am running my hand through your hair. Very softly.
JULIA: Well I guess it's alright.
ZASTROZZI: You have a very soft neck.
JULIA: Are you touching my neck? *(She looks at him)*
ZASTROZZI: Please just look ahead. *(He looks at her)* Please.
JULIA: Alright. *(She turns away)*
ZASTROZZI: Very soft neck. Very soft shoulders too. And if I may just lower my hand a little.
JULIA: Please sir.
ZASTROZZI: I'm sorry you spoke too late. Yes, your breast is also soft. But firm.
JULIA: Please. No one has ever -
ZASTROZZI: Both breasts so wonderfully firm. And my face so nice against your neck. If I could just reach down.
JULIA: No sir -
ZASTROZZI: You should have said so earlier. Your stomach. My God. This is such a wonderful feeling, isn't it?
JULIA: I'm not quite -
ZASTROZZI: That's it. Lean back a little.
JULIA: I shouldn't be doing this. *(She does nothing. She will do nothing)*
ZASTROZZI: Back a little farther. Lie down.
JULIA: All the way?
ZASTROZZI: Yes.
JULIA: But.
ZASTROZZI: Lie down.
JULIA: Like this?
ZASTROZZI: Yes.
JULIA: What are you doing now?
ZASTROZZI: Kissing you on your mouth.
(Pause)
JULIA: Yes. And now?
(Pause)
ZASTROZZI: Your breasts.
(Pause)
JULIA: Yes. And now?
(Pause)
ZASTROZZI: Relax.
(Pause)
JULIA: Yes.
(Blackout)